The Edge of the Bed

To Lydia,
Here's to a future
of adventure...
Thanks for joining
in...

xo
Lisa Palac

The Edge of the Bed

HOW DIRTY PICTURES CHANGED MY LIFE

Lisa Palac

LITTLE, BROWN AND COMPANY

BOSTON   NEW YORK   TORONTO   LONDON

First Edition

Due to the sensitive nature of the topics discussed,
the identities and certain details about some individuals have been
modified to protect their anonymity.
Portions of this book have previously appeared in *Next: Young American Writers
on the New Generation* (W.W. Norton) and the *Village Voice.*

Library of Congress Cataloging-in-Publication Data
Palac, Lisa.
The edge of the bed : how dirty pictures changed my life / Lisa Palac. — 1st ed.
p. cm.
ISBN 0-316-68849-5
1. Palac, Lisa. 2. Pornography — United States — Case studies.
3. Women — United States — Sexual behavior — Case studies.
4. Computer sex — United States — Case studies. 5. Sex oriented periodicals —
United States — Employees — Biography. I. Title.
HQ472.U6P35 1998
306.7′082 — dc21
97-45118

10 9 8 7 6 5 4 3 2 1

MV-NY

Published simultaneously in Canada by Little, Brown & Company
(Canada) Limited

Printed in the United States of America

Acknowledgments

WRITING THIS BOOK HAS been, without a doubt, the hardest thing I've ever done in my life. It is a project I couldn't have completed without the love and support of the people closest to me, who encouraged me when I felt like giving up, helped me down from some pretty shaky towers of logic and who also let me reveal many intimate details of their own lives in this book. My deepest gratitude to:

Susie Bright, for everything. Best friend, mentor, colleague, confidant, survivor of tewwible accidents and all-around genius. She is one of the greatest inspirations of my life.

Andrew Rice, for loving me beyond words, always reminding me to be fierce and teaching me how to remain calm in the face of disaster. Thanks to his red pen, readers of this book have been spared the sentence "A peep was not made by them."

Dorothy Atcheson, for her invaluable editorial insight, patience, wit and, of course, her purview.

Ron Gompertz, for his generosity and friendship, and Stephen Hadley, for opening my eyes.

I am also deeply grateful to my kick-ass agent, Sloan Harris, and my gold-star editor, Amanda Murray.

Special thanks to everyone whom I interviewed for this book, who answered questions, read early drafts and helped out in so many other ways: Laura Miller, David Pescovitz, Greg Graeff, Michael Krasny, Daryl-Lynn Johnson, Allison Diamond, Betty Dodson, Joy Johnson, Michael Johnson, Evan Sornstein, Richard Kadrey, Rob Tannenbaum, Ira Levine, Jed Emerson, Ann Powers, Danyel Smith, Gary Kamiya, Jack Morin, Joani Blank, Julene Snyder, Matisse, Bill Tonelli, Mike Godwin, Eli Sagiv, Andrew Goodwin, Joe Gore, Robert Christgau, Carola Dibbel, Stacy Horn, Dan Von Behren and Whitney Ward.

Last but not least I want to thank my family, for loving me no matter what.

Introduction

I MET LISA PALAC because I was starved for good writing. Not just any writing, nor any small appetite, either, because I was on the literary equivalent of a unicorn hunt — I was looking for women erotic writers, women who could tell you a great story and turn you on with their female experience, and that kind of woman didn't seem to exist.

In 1987, when I first began professionally to search for contributors to a women's anthology of erotica, my publisher and I had to plead, and even pray, to find authors. Our book, the one destined to launch the notorious *Herotica* series, was the bleakest project imaginable, as most writers we approached were either insulted, embarrassed or, at best, amused. There was *no* contemporary erotic fiction from women in the corner bookstore, that's for sure. I would hear from readers, particularly feminists, asking for female-point-of-view porn all the time, but the best I could suggest was something Anaïs Nin wrote sixty years ago. Or collections of women's fantasies that were pathologized by pop psychologists. Or tiny volumes by writers who spent more time apologizing for writing erotica than actually writing it.

Women were scared shitless of writing about their sexual lives in ways that didn't portray them as victims or props. The most professional authors were sure that candor about their sexual imagination would only invite mockery of their careers and intelligence. To a certain degree, they were right — the prejudice is strong that writing erotica is the equivalent of a dumb blonde making a fool of herself. But I wasn't just looking for hot prose; I wanted articulate defiance.

One day I got a manuscript from someone named Lisa LaBia (aka Miss Palac) in Chicago, with the title "Jane's Train." Jane's little sex ride on the "L" made no apologies and took no prisoners, and its author clearly delighted in her sexual bravado and humor. I nearly cried with gratitude. I remember taking the manuscript home with me and giving my lover a dramatic reading from the bathtub. Maybe there were women out there with guts, who weren't going to be shamed into self-censoring. I had to meet Lisa Palac, and when I did, it was like being introduced to a fountain of inspiration.

My biggest surprise in reading this book, as Lisa shared her final manuscript with me, was that she was so vulnerable when she first arrived in San Francisco and we began our adventures together. I saw only her determination and fearlessness — she made me feel fierce and protected when I otherwise would have hidden or surrendered. In tandem, though, we were flinchless.

It's hard to explain now, when women's candor and charisma about their sexuality are so widely admired, that not so long ago the exact same attitude would have gotten you nothing but grief, disrepute and the occasional threat to your life. When I was first editing the blatantly pornographic and feminist magazine *On Our Backs* in the early 1980s, one of the most prominent women publishers in the country called our staff to deliver the word that everyone she knew thought we ought to be "assassinated." And she wasn't kidding! There were many times when Lisa and our tiny band of comrades felt as if we were on trial at Salem. I never saw Lisa hesitate. She could take whatever the critics were dishing out, and serve it back to them on fire.

So what do veterans of the late-twentieth-century sex wars do when they get a taste of victory? Well, for one, their appetite only increases. If sexual liberation for women was just about finding the right vibrator or publishing a stroke book for chicks, we all would have tired of it a long time ago. There are quite a few books, movies and other public testimonies to women's healthy libidos these days, but I still think of us as virgins, politically, with just the first taste of truth-telling beyond titillation and adolescent rebellion. I was thrilled when Lisa told me she was going to tackle her end of our erotic revolution, because there's more to this story than a wink and a nod, and it will influence women's lives for a long time to come.

I personally won't be satisfied until every virgin-and-whore vituperation has bitten the dust, until sexual honesty is respected without caveats. Lisa gave that to me personally the first day I met her, and I am still grateful.

Susie Bright
Spring 1998

**This book is dedicated
to my mother**

The Edge of the Bed

Prologue

I **NEVER MASTURBATED OR** had an orgasm until a vibrator fell on my head when I was twenty years old. I took it as a sign.

My story unfolds like a pornographic version of *Chicken Little*. I had just moved into my very first low-rent apartment and was on tiptoes dusting a high closet shelf when a small rubber object fell from the sky and bonked me. My college roommate, Sooze, and I both stared at this thing on the floor, then slightly backed away from it like it was radioactive. It was flesh-colored and shaped vaguely like a fat Christmas tree. There was a white wire that came out of the base and attached to a battery pack.

"What is it?"

"I think it's some kind of . . . vibrator."

"Gross."

I'd read about vibrators before but had never actually seen one up close. I immediately flashed on where this item must have been and the fact that it fell *on my head*. Neither of us wanted to pick it up, but soon we were laughing so hard, we couldn't do much of anything. Finally we scooped it up into a shoe box and decided we would exhibit it at our next party as a gag. We hid the vibrator under the sink in the bathroom and made sure the toilet paper was just about to run out. A search in the obvious places for a new roll inevitably led to a sighting of it. Hilarious.

I found these types of practical jokes so amusing that I lugged the vibrator with me as I moved from apartment to apartment. Then one day I decided the joke was getting old. As I was dangling the vibrator over the trash can, inspiration appeared like a cartoon bubble above my head with these words: *Try It.*

I did everything but boil the thing to ensure I wouldn't contract a disease. I turned the vibrator on and set it down on the bed, as a test. In my paranoid state, it sounded like a lawn mower. Leaving the vibrator running, I piled lots of blankets on top of it and walked out of the room to see if I could hear it. The faint buzzing *could* be interpreted as a blender. I could put some music on, which would cover up the buzz, but then I wouldn't be able to hear my roommate when she came home. If she busted me playing with myself, well, the humiliation would be unspeakable.

Suddenly the whole experiment started to get so complicated I was tempted to forget it. So before I chickened out, I tore off my clothes and lay down. I couldn't figure out why the thing was shaped so oddly, like a rubber Popsicle with these three ridges that increased in diameter. Was I supposed to put it inside or outside or what? *I can't believe I am so dumb I don't know how to use a vibrator.*

Despite the fact that I was alone, I was extremely self-conscious. I decided to put it between my legs and move it around on the outside first and see what happened. In a matter of seconds, maybe sixty, I felt something. It was the same sensation I once got doing The Bicycle in an aerobics class; the same tingly feeling I once woke up with after a psychedelic wet dream about making out with my boyfriend. But those sensations had been random; I didn't know how to stir them up on command. This sensation on my clitoris was directly related to the machine in my right hand, and it was much more than a tiny tingle. And then I came.

"Jesus," I thought, as I peeled myself off the ceiling, "so *that's* the Big O I'm always reading about in *Cosmo*."

It was about time, too. How could it have taken me twenty years?

• • •

These days, whenever someone asks me the inevitable cocktail question, "What do you do?" I give them the straightforward yet morally neutral and conveniently abstract answer: "I'm a writer." It's the truth, but not exactly the whole truth. In the years since that rubber object fell from the sky, I've worked as a sex magazine editor, an erotic multimedia producer, a freelance journalist covering sexual politics and a writer of countless *Penthouse*-style letters. I've been called the Queen of High-Tech Sex, a Do Me Feminist and a Sex-Positive Feminist Pornographer, among other things. Of course, a few of these titles were self-selected. When I got my first official editorial job at a hard-core sex magazine, I got a big kick out of answering The Question with "I'm a pornographer." I was trying pretty hard to prove that even nice corn-fed midwestern girls could be interested in the sexually explicit. But eventually I decided that blasting people off their chairs with the "shocking" truth about my professional life wasn't an approach that should be used indiscriminately in every social situation. Frankly, I didn't want to shock people — the word *pornography* did it almost every time — since most of them already listed shock as one of their primary responses to the discussion of sex. I wanted them to relax and feel like talking about sex could be done with the same candor and relevance as talking about art, music, travel, the sunrise or any other topic that comes up over dinner. And so I began checking the less confrontational box marked writer.

Naturally, my answer to The Question is always followed by "So, what do you write about?"

"Sex," I say, without rushing to cover it up with a nervous laugh.

From here the conversation can take a number of different directions. A few pie-eyed people will completely change the subject or even politely excuse themselves. A few more will crack jokes like *Sex? You must have a lot of experience.* Heh heh. Or *Sex? Now there's a subject I know something about!* Wink wink. But most people? They sincerely *go off.* They want to exchange opinions on sex toys, S/M, erotica, anal sex, cybersex — you name it. They want to ask a million questions — the ones they've always been too embarrassed to ask — about sexual fantasies, positions and health. Ultimately, courageously, they want to spill their sexual secrets. It is with great interest and a soft heart that I listen to their personal confessions — which so often end with "I've never told anyone that before" — because I have spent much of my adult life examining my sexual conscience in public. Telling the whole world things I've never told anyone before.

One of the most popular questions people ask is "How did you get so interested in sex?" I tell them I was raised Catholic. We all have a good yuk over that one. Ah, Catholicism. Where sex is dirty and the thrill of transgression is endless! While there's no denying that my religious upbringing certainly influenced my sexual attitudes, it was hardly the only factor. My parents, popular culture, feminism, anti-porn ideology, digital technology and the sexual intelligentsia of San Francisco all made priceless contributions. But the most truthful answer to the question is also the simplest one: Because everyone is interested in sex. Those three little letters suck us into their vortex so fast, even the most jaded and cynical are unable to resist anything with the word *SEX* printed on it. Acknowledging our sexual interest, though, is never easy. How can it be when sex is at once trivial, pivotal, disgusting, beautiful, embarrassing, empowering and the reason we're all here?

This book is a document of my own sexual journey, of my erotic interests and cultural observations. I've written it because I believe that honesty encourages honesty. Telling the truth about sex — the most intimate, contradiction-filled, hard-to-be-honest-about subject of them all — has given me the courage to face the rest of my complicated life as honestly as I can.

I believe I'm a better person because of — not in spite of — all the sex I've been exposed to. The sexual images and ideas thrown at me by rock and roll, porn, television, Hollywood movies and cyberspace have ultimately left me feeling more liberated than oppressed, more enlightened than frightened. Occasionally someone will pick a fight with me, asking pointy questions like "What about snuff films?" or "What about kids looking at porn on the Internet? Let's see you try to put your little sex-positive spin on that!" While I do, in fact, have my spins on these sorts of questions (all of which are in this book), I have no interest in seeing human sexuality as a globe of perfection, in always looking on the bright side. Everybody knows the world is not an eternally cheerful place where life is beautiful all the time. Why should our erotic world be an exception? It's easy to fall back on aphorisms like "Our culture is so afraid of sex" as a way of explaining my fears. But the truth is, I am wary of sex. Of its transformative powers, its troublesome spells. Flames of passion, hot sex, molten lust, burning desire — it all sounds very poetic except for the fact that actually being on fire is terribly painful.

Learning to speak the truth about sex, trying to figure out how — or if — my erotic desires can be reconciled with my politics, finding the spiritual places where physical intimacy takes me — these are some of the most important things I've ever done. But I'm no sex expert. I don't have a secret sex handshake or magic X-ray glasses. What I know came from my dogged determination to look at and talk about the things I wasn't supposed to — even though most of them had been shoved right under my nose.

Climbing trees of knowledge has taught me many things, including this: The rubber object that fell out of the closet wasn't a vibrator exactly — it was a butt-plug. It may have taken twenty years and an appliance to put sexual pleasure in the palm of my hand, but I've sure made up for lost time.

1

Birth of a Love Child

WHILE ON A BUSINESS trip to Rome, my father visited the Vatican, where, struck by grace, he fell to his knees and begged God to save his marriage. Inspired, he flew home to my mother in Chicago and made — as she later described it — mad, passionate love to her. Their bedroom valor was short-lived but the consequences were not. My mother, age thirty-eight, was pregnant — seventeen years after her first daughter was born.

I was born on November 4, 1963. The same day the Beatles played for the Queen of England, eighteen days before John F. Kennedy was assassinated and a few months after the massive civil rights demonstration in Washington, D.C., where Martin Luther King Jr. declared, "I have a dream." Millions of people were able to watch the march live on television because of Telestar II, the first successful communications satellite launched into space that same year — a media revolution. By 1963, an estimated 2.3 million women were on the Pill and Betty Friedan's *Feminine Mystique* was on the bestseller list. It was the year the words *sexual revolution* became the metaphor of choice to describe America's changing sexual attitudes, winning out over descriptions like "morals revolution" and "sexplosion."

My father's name was Florian Francis, which he abbreviated for business purposes to F.F., which led his devoted children to call him *ffff ffff* and frequently, The F'er. He held a variety of high-rolling executive jobs, and every morning he left for work wearing a sharp suit; briefcase in one hand, a Winston in the other. He drove off in his Buick Electra 225 and rarely came home for supper. Both of my parents had grown up poor, and neither went to college, yet my father had no shortage of loud back-slappers for success like "Grab the world by the ass!" and "Don't piss all over your shoes!" Whenever we went out to dinner, he always left a huge tip for the waitress, and was fond of describing women as "sexy broads." The basement of our house was his refuge, his place to crack open a bottle of Dewar's and carry on. Every once in a while he'd pretend to be opera star Mario Lanza at full volume. My mother would make a horrible face and say, "Your father's blasting away again down there!"

My mother, Arlene, drove an Electrolux. She stayed at home, raised the children and engaged in an uninterrupted cycle of housecleaning. Notes were taped to the walls instructing us to "Take off shoes!" and "Wipe down walls after shower!" All of our furniture was covered in plastic. She vacuumed the carpet so all of the nap went in the same direction. She mowed the lawn with golf-course precision. She went to church every Tuesday night and prayed to Saint Anthony. She also loved telling dirty jokes, cocktail parties and smoking menthol cigarettes while she gossiped on the phone. Trips to the beauty parlor and shopping for the latest fashions were also high-ranking activities. Everything had to match: her shoes, her purse, her lipstick, her pants. When she left the house, she always looked beautiful. At night she slept perfectly still, with her arms crossed over her chest like a dead person, so she wouldn't mess up her hairdo.

My childhood was like any other. I was Cinderella in the kindergarten play. I took tap and ballet lessons. I was a Brownie, then a Girl Scout. I was the second girl in my fifth-grade class to grow breasts, but to the older boys in the neighborhood, I was still just fat and four-eyed. I was so much younger than my sister and two brothers — who were, respectively, seventeen, fifteen and eight years older than me — that by the time I reached puberty I was on my own.

I'll never forget the day I ran down the stairs in the nude to show my mother my first pubic hair. Do you know why I will never forget this day? Because my mother still talks about it to every manicurist and Hallmark card shop attendant in the greater Chicagoland area. "This is my baby, my *darling* Lisa," she says, introducing me and squeezing my arm. "Oh, I still remember the day she ran down the stairs in the nude to show me her first pubic hair!"

Today I have a portrait of my mother taken in 1944, when she was just seventeen, hanging in my office. Everyone tells me I look exactly like her, which I find flattering and terrifying at the same time.

Her sexual attractiveness is something my mother has always taken great pride in. She loves to tell the story of how, in 1945, she was the second runner-up in the Yankee Girl beauty contest at the Chicago Stadium. Or how movie star

Tyrone Power once asked her to dance, choosing her above all the others at a fancy ballroom soiree. Or how she had so many handsome (wealthy, even divorced!) boyfriends before my father. "I was a sexpot too when I was your age!" she frequently reminds me. She was no prude but when it came to my sexuality and discussing it in an appropriate, matter-of-fact way, she, like so many parents, didn't know how to do it.

Some time after the arrival of my pubic hair, my mother and I were on one of our slow-motion Saturday shopping trips where she had never-ending conversations with the store clerks while I wandered around pressing my face against the glass display counters until the manager would ask me to please stop that. Every time I'd try to speed things along, she'd say, "I am in no hurry to go back to my prison." As a reward for simply bearing witness to the passage of time, I got to pick out a little treat for myself. I held out my selection and said, "I want this." It was a paperback titled, *Everything You Always Wanted to Know About Sex — But Were Afraid to Ask.* She wrinkled up her face and gave me her famous look of righteous criticism, the one that wordlessly conveys the sentiment "*That?* I would never pick *that!*" I responded with my own look of "Just hurry up and pay for it because I haven't got all day." She tossed the book on the checkout counter and slowly exhaled while she shook her head. The slow exhale + head shake always meant, in perpetuity, "I have sacrificed my life for my children. And this? This is the way they treat me."

Every child is curious about sex, but I've always had a special talent for asking the most intimate questions. I once asked one of my older brothers if he wiped after he peed. He looked at me like I was a moron. One Christmas Eve, when our entire family was walking to midnight Mass, I suddenly felt the urge to cross-reference the information in my new book. I turned to my then sister-in-law and quite loudly asked her, "What's an orgasm?" Before she could answer, I heard my mother gasp, "Ojésus kochany!" (Polish for "O my sweet Jesus.") "On the way to church!"

The *Everything You Always Wanted to Know . . .* sex book was just the beginning. While other kids were reading the classics or out experiencing nature, I was watching *Love, American Style,* rocking out to Led Zeppelin and reading *Go Ask Alice* over and over. The places I expected to learn about sex — in school, from my parents, at church — I didn't, and I quickly realized that popular culture was *the* place to get a sex education. Of course, nobody on my block called it *popular culture.* Top 40 radio, trashy paperbacks, sitcoms and Hollywood movies were simply *that crap* we all couldn't get enough of.

For me, the crème de la crap included an old 45 of the Beatles' "I Saw Her Standing There." I loved the 1-2-3-4! countdown before the guitars rushed in and Paul sang, *Well she was just seventeen/You know what I mean.* Well, I didn't know what he meant. It would take me years to understand the sexual significance of seventeen-year-old girls. In the meantime, I jumped up and down and sang along because it felt good. Music, like sex itself, lets us feel things before we can spell them.

Even though rock songs blatantly described plenty of sexual acts — like girls who never lost their head even when they were giving head — the lyrics were only a small part of the information package. It was the cultural phenomenon of rock — the lifestyle of the stars, their performances, the gossip, the groupies, the album covers and the ineffable, transformative power of the music, inseparable from the lyrics and the way they were sung — that taught me about the whole human sexual drama. The grade-school rumors, for instance, that "David Bowie is gay *and* bisexual!" or "Neil Sedaka is gay with Elton John!" introduced me to the very idea of homosexuality and the queer life. Everything about Jimi Hendrix shored up my assumption that black people were just naturally sexier than white people. From his monumental guitar sound to the Plaster Casters' immortalization of his big black cock, Hendrix was *the* icon of black male sexuality in my segregated white-girl world and represented all that I feared and wondered about black men.

Until I became a rock fan, I'd always pictured masculinity and femininity as two distinct fixed points on opposite ends of the scale, inseparable from being male or female. Women were feminine and men were masculine and that was that. Then along came a guy named Alice Cooper and I thought, That can't be right. Everybody knows Alice is a girl's name. Rock turned the Beaver Cleaver notions of gender inside out. Rock stars were doing all the things good girls weren't sup-posed to do — wearing wild, sleazy outfits, rubbing their asses and wagging their tongues and acting like sluts who want sex NOW! — except most of them were boys. At the time, men wearing lipstick and high heels seemed like nothing more than zany, rock star antics to me. Now I see that those antics ex-posed me to a cornerstone idea of modern sexual philosophy: Gender is a construct. Our sex is something we're born with, we're either male or female. But our gender, our sense of mas-culinity or feminity, is something we acquire. How to be a man, how to act ladylike — these are things anyone can learn.

Like music, television — in addition to being my babysitter, dinner date, humanities professor, political adviser and late-night companion — was another sexual secret agent. TV slipped me coded bits of data: make-out scenes that faded to black, the faux hilarity of saying "make whoopee," go-go girls in bikinis and naked men hiding in closets right next to Miss Jane Hathaway. An advertisement for the Mark Eden Bust Developer featured zaftig bombshells in polyester midriffs stretching tape measures across their giant boobs. (I dreaded the very thought of wearing a bra, and so the horror remained: Why would anyone want big ones?) As a regular bit on *The Sonny and Cher Comedy Hour,* Cher, always in red, sprawled on top of an upright piano and sang the praises of being a v-a-m-p-vamp! In fact, Cher broke a long-standing TV taboo when she showed America her bellybutton. More important, she presented herself as both a sexual being *and* a mom, a radical concept then and now.

Pop culture glued me to my friends, expanded my vocabulary and, of course, tipped me off to the big world of sexual possibilities. It was the type of sex education where I learned through suggestion and nuance. But if I wanted more than nuance, all I had to do was dig through the neighbor's trash to find it, or under my older brothers' beds, or in the basement where my father had a couple copies of *Hustler* hidden above his fishing tackle. Whenever I'd start to feel bored and there was nothing to do, I'd perk myself up by thinking, "Maybe I should go look at that *Hustler* magazine again." Back then, the only thing I knew about pornography was that it was bad and I better not get caught looking at it. So on hot summer days when nobody was around, I'd go downstairs, lie on the cool concrete floor and look at the beaver shots. There was one photo of an Asian woman smoking a cigarette out of her pussy. At the time, it was the most bizarre thing I ever saw.

• • •

The year I turned fifteen I decided it was time to get some hands-on educational experience. It was the year all hell broke loose.

My eighteen-year-old boyfriend, James V., took me to the next dimension in his '72 Charger. The first thing I did before he picked me up from my all-girl Catholic high school was to change out of my gross school uniform and into jeans so tight I had to lie down and zip them up with a pair of pliers. I also took off my thick glasses so he wouldn't see me in them, which left me practically blind, and if I'd had the tools, I would have taken the braces off my teeth, too. My hair was long and stack-permed, my face weighted down with purple eyeshadow and roll-on fruit-flavored lip gloss. I accessorized with marijuana jewelry.

Next came these incredible make-out sessions in his car, where he'd finger me for hours and I'd go crazy. Every time we started to kiss, he turned into a human sprinkler, with sweat spouting from every pore in his body. I took this as a sign — he's so hot for me! — and often hinted that if he wanted to, you know, go all the way, I'd be up for that. But no. He kept his distance. "I don't think we feel the same way about this relationship," he once told me. I desperately wanted to lose my virginity, just to see what the big fuss was all about but, clearly, he didn't want the job.

One night when I thought I had the house to myself, I

invited James over for a session. I closed the door to my bedroom and cranked up Cheap Trick. Our shirts were off and
our pants were down when I heard a loud knock. The regret-
tably unlocked door swung open, and my father switched on
the light. I watched his face go from "Hi, honey, I'm home"
to "Jesus Fucking Christ" in a matter of seconds. He didn't
say a word. He slammed the door and went downstairs.

"Ohgod, ohgod, ohgod." James was now frantic. "Oh god,
your father's gonna kill me." He continued to whine "gonna
kill me" under his breath as he pulled his pants up and scrambled to get dressed. "Should I jump out the window?"

"Just follow me downstairs and act normal," I said.

"Should I blow-dry my hair first? This looks really bad,"
he said, looking into the mirror and running a hand over his
sweat-soaked head.

"My dad's cool. Don't worry."

"You sure?"

I gave him a look of utter confidence that masked my true
suspicions, because that's what I wanted — for my father to
be cool about it.

We walked downstairs and through the kitchen, where my
Dad was making himself a headcheese sandwich. We were almost to the back door — free and clear — when my father
said, quite politely, "Excuse me, young man. Can I talk to you
for a minute?"

James turned and walked toward my father, who put a
gentle arm around James's shoulder and began to pontificate
on male sexual desire. "I understand what it's like to be a
young man. To want to sow your wild oats . . ."

Sow your wild oats? Oh man, you're so square. I chuckled
silently and began to feel all the muscles in my body relax.

". . . And if you were my son, I would applaud you for what you just did. . . ."

I was right. Everything's cool.

". . . But you're not my son. So if I EVER catch you trying to DEFLOWER my daughter again, I'll BREAK . . . your FUCKING . . . NECK." With one swift move, my father had him by the collar, up against the wall. James's feet were dangling a few inches off the floor.

"Yes, Mr. Palac." James was gasping for air.

I began screaming and pleading and pounding on my father to stop until he let go. James slumped to his knees but quickly shifted his position and sprinted for the back door, never to be seen again. Without a word, my father went back to making his sandwich.

"Daddy, it's not what you think. We weren't . . ." I collapsed on the shiny green kitchen floor that my mother religiously waxed. "I didn't let him . . . He didn't even *want* to!" My father didn't say anything, but I knew what he was thinking.

"I'm not a whore!" I sobbed. He stepped over me and carried his sandwich on a paper plate down into the basement.

My mother's response to my early sexual experimentation generally wasn't much better. Once, after she caught me Frenching a boy in our living room, she paraded around the house with the back of her hand to her forehead shrieking, "The way you were *kissing* and *embracing!*" She kept spitting out the words *kissing* and *embracing* over and over like poison until I was so filled with shame that I broke down and begged for forgiveness. For weeks afterward she was on the phone to her friends, filling them in on my big sin.

I suspect it was my parents' inability to honestly deal with their own erotic desires that caused them to act so hysterical about mine. Their libidos orbited around each other like two separate universes. I never once saw my parents kiss each other out of passion, although there was the occasional obligatory peck at family gatherings. I never stood outside my parents' bedroom door and listened for intimate sounds because there was no such thing as my parents' bedroom. From the time I was three, they slept in separate rooms. I shared a king-size bed with my mother until I was twelve years old, old enough to demand my own space. While other children were traumatized by their parents' divorce and did all sorts of stunts to keep them together, I always prayed that my parents would wise up and split up, because I couldn't stand their constant fighting. But they considered themselves good Catholics, and divorce was unthinkable.

For me, Catholicism was fourteen long years of ugly plaid uniforms, confessing to empty boxfuls of sin and silently debating whether Mary stayed a virgin even after Jesus was born. I'd stare up at the crucifix and wonder how much it must have hurt. Then I'd wonder what Jesus looked like naked. Age twelve: As part of a faith-affirming church sacrament, I choose Magdalene as my confirmation name, as in Mary Magdalene, as in great whore of the New Testament, the thirteenth disciple of Jesus. Coincidence or prophecy?

Because of my profane thoughts, I feared that I'd become a nun, as a punishment. That would straighten me out but good. On Career Day at school, joining the convent was always presented as a fine choice. "But not everyone is chosen to do the Lord's work," the sisters would say, and go on to tell us how one day they just "got the calling" and that was that. "God, please don't pick me," I'd whisper over and over, bowing my head. Eventually I realized my chances of getting into a religious order were slim because I'd blown the vows of poverty and obedience. Chastity, however, still hung over my adolescent head like a threat, but I took care of that soon enough.

The first time I had sex was one of the biggest disappointments of my life. After James came Tom, another eighteen-year-old guy who worked full-time in an auto parts store. Our relationship was dull and brief, lasting only a month or two. We did it in his grandmother's bed.

"Where's your grandmother?" I asked him.

"Oh, she died last week."

Just before the big moment, I admitted that I didn't *exactly* know what to do. "Just open your legs and rock," he told me, which sounded remarkably like a Foghat song. It was over in minutes. Afterwards, I was extremely disappointed and felt sick with guilt. I kept torturing myself with the mantra "I am not a virgin I am not a virgin," which was stupid because I'd done practically everything else — as many of the other girls in my class had done — yet none of that constituted sex. It wasn't sex until he put it in.

By the time I officially learned the word *clitoris* during my sophomore year at Resurrection High, I'd been having sexual intercourse for six months. (My sister, bless her progressive soul, took me to her gynecologist and got me started on the Pill.) Mrs. Pancratz, my very attractive gym teacher, gave us the basic sperm-and-egg lesson, an explanation of the menstrual cycle and pointed out the clitoris on a larger-than-life diagram of the vulva. Stimulation of the clitoris, she said, had only one purpose: to provide sexual pleasure. She pronounced it cli-TOR-is, which definitely sounded retarded and threw the class into snorty, suppressed fits of laughter. I thought it should be pronounced CLITTER-is. More important, I thought, how come I never heard of this clitoris before? And if it's supposed to give me sexual pleasure, then how come the boys I had sex with never mentioned it, much less touched it? The thought that I could touch it never even occurred to me. Hard to believe that a girl as curious about sex as I was would sit there thinking, *Clitoris . . . the pleasure button . . . hmmm, I guess I'll file that tidbit of physiology away right next to the purpose of the medulla oblongata.* But I did.

While my girlfriends and I traded boy secrets — who we thought was cute, who we let feel us up, who we did it with — we were all in unspoken agreement that only guys played with themselves. Those losers. Even if we wanted to crack jokes about girls and masturbation, there weren't any words for it. Boys called each other "jag-offs," but there was no female equivalent. If there was any jerking, beating, stroking or jagging off to be done, it involved a penis, not a clitoris. The absence of any such descriptive language — then and now — is a testament to how cut off women are from their sexuality, both physically and psychologically.

Despite all the sex clues hidden in pop culture, I came across absolutely nothing about female masturbation. Led Zeppelin sure wasn't singing about the clitoris, and there was no episode of *The Brady Bunch* where Marcia finds her clit and comes. Even in the sex magazines I saw, women just spread their legs, they didn't touch, and it gave me the impression that just spreading would result in a deep state of ecstasy. While seventies feminism and books like Betty Dodson's *Liberating Masturbation* (a how-to manual published in 1974) honored the vagina and encouraged women to talk more openly about their sexuality, feminism didn't make the rounds at my high school or in my family. I never even heard the word *feminist* until I got to college. If an idea wasn't reflected in the world I defined myself by — if the radio didn't play it and movies didn't show it and TV didn't mention it and my peers didn't talk about it, it wasn't cool. And if it wasn't cool, forget it.

I believed that sexual satisfaction was something I lay back and waited for. An orgasm was something my boyfriend gave to me — only he didn't. I remember my true teenage love, Billy, once asking me the inevitable question after intercourse, "Did you come?" Embarrassingly, I said I didn't — ever. "Don't you masturbate to come?" he asked. I gave him my own look of righteous criticism: *That?* I would never do *that!* He spent the next hour with his head between my legs, paying full attention to my clit, but my performance anxiety was so high that — for the first and last time — I faked an orgasm. I didn't want him to feel bad after all that work.

● ● ●

Unlike most other all-girl Catholic high schools in the city, Resurrection didn't have a nearby all-boys high school, which resulted in the neighborhood chant: Go to Res and be a lez! Most of us, however, simply ended up in heterosexual relationships with junkies, felons and other exciting lowlifes. Such was the effect of sexual segregation and a protectionist mentality. There was no sanctioned outlet for all of our pent-up sexual energy. No captain of the football team to chase after, not even a few pimply geek-boys to experiment with. The limited supply of auto parts clerks and schoolmates' brothers dried up quickly. Where were we supposed to meet guys?

I met them by hanging out in front of the 7-Eleven and asking the cute ones to buy me a six-pack. When I was just seventeen, my girlfriends and I would drive around in my father's Cadillac on Friday nights looking for excitement. We found it, all right — a bunch of white guys in their twenties who were all on their way in or out of prison. Everything about their scene was so fascinating, so bad-ass! They had tattoos, they listened to this crazy new music called rap and, most important, they loved to party and get in our pants.

My father often said to me, "If Jesus Christ Himself were to come down from heaven and ask me for your hand in marriage, I don't know if He'd be good enough for you!" It was a decision he would never have to make. I fell in love with Mario. He was twenty-six, had a significant criminal record and a heroin problem to match, but I couldn't help but believe that he was a really good person deep down inside, especially when we were both snuggling on the couch and sucking our thumbs. I clung to my "good-person" belief even on the day I walked into my own house and saw contrary evidence: the contents of every drawer, closet and bureau emptied out all over the floor, picked clean of the valuables. Furs, silver, china, my mother's wedding ring, all of it gone.

My uncle, a Chicago detective, came over with a pile of mug shots. Mario's picture was on top. As my uncle flipped through the stack, he would ask me, "Do you know this crook?" I answered yes almost every time. My father was pacing back and forth, teeth clenched, the ash from his cigarette dropping right onto the carpet. I felt ashamed for getting involved with such a delinquent crowd, but mostly I felt like walking out the door and never coming back. By this time, my father was spending increasing amounts of time in the basement, drinking. After years of following the formula for the American Dream (hard work = success) my father had been betrayed by it. He'd been squeezed out in a company merger. For a long time he remained unemployed, with fifty-eight years of experience nobody seemed to want. My mother spent increasing amounts of time in bed, and would end up being hospitalized for severe depression over and over again. My siblings had all left home years ago, and I was sick of swimming alone in the churning water.

Mario once showed me a Polaroid of himself standing on a steep hill in San Francisco, taken when he broke parole and ran to the West Coast, where he worked in a bakery in North Beach with a bunch of old Italian ladies. Eventually he got busted and sent back to Joliet State Penitentiary, but in the picture he was smiling, holding on to the pole of a yellow warning sign that read, "Hill." The ground dipped behind him and disappeared. It looked as if he was standing on the edge of the world. California, I thought, is the place I oughtta be.

My first dream of going west was quashed when my father refused to send me to the University of California, Berkeley. "How will you get home for Christmas and all the other family holidays? I'm not busting my ass for the airfare!" he shouted. My thoughts exactly.

I ended up completing one year of premed at Loyola University in Chicago. The following year I moved to Minneapolis and enrolled at the University of Minnesota, this time applying to the School of Nursing. I wanted to be a midwife. My father viewed college as vocational training and I felt obligated to choose a career that would recoup all that tuition. Business, medicine or law — the trinity of success. I also wanted to make it all up to my father, to ameliorate all of my screw-ups — namely, the Jailbird Incident — and get the one thing I always pretended I didn't need: his respect. So I tried to walk the high wire between my own aspirations and my father's expectations, but destiny got in my way.

2

How Dirty Pictures Changed My Life

"**B**URN IT," I SAID. I pointed at the stockpile of hard-core porn that had just avalanched out of the closet. "Burn every last bit of it. Or it's over." If looks could kill, my college boyfriend, Greg Graeff, would have dropped dead. I had opened the door to get a sweater and got a glossy, four-color mountain of pussy instead.

"How could *you* — Mr. Sensitive Guy —" I mocked him, "enjoy looking at this disgusting crap?" Oh, I was livid. I paced around his tiny one-room apartment, spitting venom, devising his punishment. "Either all this sleazy shit goes or I go."

He stood still and looked at me as if he was about to cry, his fingers nervously picking at the edges of his flannel shirt. "I'll get rid of it all, I promise," he whispered. Silence. "But first if I could just show you . . . if you would watch just one video with me?" The nerve. He prattled on about how he just wanted a chance to explain why this stuff turned him on and that it didn't mean he didn't love me and if I didn't like it he would, yes, destroy it all. I crossed my arms and chewed on the inside of my lip for a very long minute. That evening we watched *Sleepless Nights*. It was the first dirty movie I ever saw.

Growing up, I clearly got the message that pornography was bad and I shouldn't look at it. When I went away to college, I got the same message. Only this time, it wasn't coming from the Church or my parents but from the politics of feminism.

...

I spent most of my sophomore year undergoing various incarnations: from heavy metal chick to preppie to new wave punk with pink hair. Even if I could handle the science it took to get a nursing degree, I couldn't handle the outfits. I dropped out and went to art school. I came out as a film major. My roommate, Sooze, came out as a lesbian.

Sooze was the first person I met who'd been born and raised in California — the land of my milk and honey dreams. Her distinctly SoCal character was brought to life by use of the phrase *no way* to describe every situation from looking in the refrigerator — "Orange juice, no way!" — to lousy grades — "A C+? No way!" — to my personalized greeting — "Lisa Palac, no way!" So when she told me she was gay, my response was "No way. Really?" It was my first encounter with someone who — surprise — was queer. While I acted nonchalant about her news, inside I was pretty upset by it. She might as well have just peeled her face off to reveal an alien identity. I worried that her newfound sexual identity signaled the end of our best-friendship. Would we still do goofy shit like dressing up Sooze's left arm — which ended just below her elbow, a handicap she was born with — like a Miss Piggy puppet? Or would her baby dyke lifestyle wedge itself uncomfortably in between us? Or would my own low-level homophobia push us apart?

Sooze was a Women's Studies major at the university and it was Sooze who introduced me to feminism. "Isn't it just bullshit that women are supposed to shave their armpits but men don't have to?" she'd say. I agreed and stopped shaving. My hairy pits were my first political statement. I also thought they made me look like Patti Smith, who posed elbows-up on the cover of her album *Easter*.

But deep inside the debates over whether or not to shave or wear high heels and makeup lay the heart of feminism: women's social, economic and sexual equality. Of course, it was all news to me since I was raised in a political black hole. My mother wasn't a feminist. My sister didn't call herself a feminist. I was nineteen and couldn't really tell the difference between sexy and sexist. Injustice was simply a natural event. Getting paid less than a man for the same work, enduring public comments on the size of my breasts, being valued for my beauty over my brains — I accepted it all as part of being a girl. But feminism taught me to think critically about my life as a woman in a way I'd never done before. In feminism, I found the salvation I never got from the Bible.

And when it came to exposing sexism, I was a maniac. Nothing escaped dissection under my brand-new feminist microscope. Sexism was everywhere, and my job was to root it out, out, OUT! Any use of the word *girl* to describe a woman: inexcusable violation. All Roxy Music albums featuring heavily eyeshadowed, half-naked women on the cover: enemy propaganda. Madonna? A traitorous bimbo for crawling around on the floor and wearing that embarrassing Boy Toy belt buckle. Any sexually oriented use of a woman's body to sell products or supply entertainment: the ultimate exploitation. Pornography, of course, was the supreme offender.

By 1983 Minneapolis had become a hotbed of radical antiporn politics. Catharine MacKinnon and Andrea Dworkin were teaching a class on porn at the University of Minnesota, and they drafted the very first feminist-inspired antipornography law, defining pornography as a form of sex discrimination. Over the course of the next few years, *The Story of O* was picketed on campus, with flyers denouncing S/M as just another bourgeois word for violence. *Not a Love Story,* a documentary about one woman's adverse experience in the porn business, became a Women's Studies classic. Women Against Pornography, a group of anti-porn radicals, toured the heartland with their slide show featuring the notorious *Hustler* cover of a nude woman being fed head-first through a meat grinder. A young woman set herself on fire in Shinder's Bookstore on Hennepin Avenue and left a suicide note that said, ". . . Pornographers and the values they represent have ruined my life." The message was clear: Destroy or be destroyed.

Aside from stolen glances at my father's collection, the only pornography I'd seen was in the Women's Studies classroom. This carefully selected group of pornographic images didn't appear very liberating. She's tied up and gagged, with clothespins biting down on her nipples. She's spreading her labia with her fingers while a man ejaculates on her face. They were described as *inherently* degrading and oppressive. I looked at these pictures, added my own experience of being sized up as a piece of ass and concluded that pornography was the reason women were second-class. Pornography bred sexual injustice. Like Justice Potter Stewart, I knew pornography when I saw it and I'd seen enough to rally for the cause. I chanted and marched and applauded the spray painting of LIES ABOUT WOMEN over Virginia Slims ads and over the windows of adult bookstores. I talked in slogans like, "Porn is the theory and rape is the practice." I added "anti-porn feminist" to my list of ever-mutating personae.

Since feminism and the anti-porn manifestos were presented to me simultaneously, I accepted them as a package. How could I be a feminist and *not* be against pornography? Yet deep down, I had doubts about the definition of pornography I'd been handed: that it is the number one reason women are oppressed, degraded and exploited; that it causes violence; that it *is* violence. Yes, the images I'd seen offended me, but surely there must be sexual images that weren't sexist. Where were the *good erotic* images to replace the *bad pornographic* ones? If the bottom line was that looking at pictures of people having sex was wrong, then I hadn't come very far from Catholic school after all.

I also began to wonder how the concept of "sexual objectification" fit in with what I was doing in bed. I liked it when I took off my clothes and my boyfriend told me how much my body turned him on. I liked sex and, frankly, I liked to feel my lover come all over me. I considered it an intimate sensual gift, not an act of degradation. Was I unfeminist?

Then there was that vibrator, the one that fell on my head, and the fact that I'd just started to have orgasms. What was a woman — a feminist — supposed to think about when she masturbated? Nobody talked about this. The forbidden aspect of pornography made me extremely curious, but I didn't have the guts to check it out by myself. And now my boyfriend's porn collection came tumbling out of the closet.

• • •

"Ready?"

"Yeah," my voice cracked. Greg slipped the X-rated video into the VCR.

Greg and I met when we were both art students, cocktailing at First Avenue, a Minneapolis nightclub. He was six foot four and extremely thin, with long dark hair, bad skin, big teeth and a wildly expressive face that was constantly zinging and zipping from one emotion to the next with cartoon-like speed. He also possessed the natural ability to be offensive, charming and hugely dorky all in the course of a single minute, a combination that drew women to him in an almost scientifically proven way. His approach to sex was adventurous and enthusiastic, but never pushy. We spoke openly about our erotic ideas and desires — he was the only person who knew about my vibrator exploits — and for the first few months of our relationship I believed our sex life was secret-free.

Now here we were, both nervous and cagey. He was afraid I was going to hate the video and break up with him. I was afraid of every single possibility. Sitting on the floor in front of the TV, I started imagining the worst: What if Sooze finds out about this? What if Greg tries to coerce me into doing a sex act he sees in this movie? What if I get turned on by this crap? What if I become a porn addict?

Afterward, I critiqued the film: "That was boring and stupid." Everything was bad — the acting, the lighting, the lingerie, the hair. The basics of good moviemaking, like plot and continuity, were ignored. Scene after scene featured close-up tedious sex on a pool table, on the kitchen floor, on a bed. I waited for the violent rape and torture scenes. They never happened. The film followed a lick-suck-fuck formula that ended in orgasm, not murder. Still, I was not turned on in the least.

Of course, if it was all so boring and stupid, why did I agree to watch another one? Because watching people have sex is compelling. Because I got a charge out of breaking a taboo. But mostly, because I was in love. Greg was sharing an intimate part of himself with me, trusting me not to reject him, and I wanted to understand and accept the side of him he'd so painstakingly hidden from me. Plus, his excitement about our little adventure was infectious.

Over the course of the next few screenings, I felt angry, indifferent and depressed but never turned-on. X-rated films have all the elements of Hollywood make-believe — actors read scripts, role-play, take direction — but with one big distinction: they have real sex. Because the sexual acts in porn are real, not faked, they have the power to be more of a turn-on than R-rated erotic films and more of a bummer for the exact same reason. Some of the actors looked bored, others looked strung-out. Some fucked in unnatural positions for the sake of the camera. The men were unemotional. The women were so skinny and young, I felt like shouting, "Get out of porn and run for your lives!" I imagined myself in their place. What would my family think if I did such a thing? Wouldn't all these women rather be doing something else if only they had the skill or means?

Soon, a new emotion crept into the mix: superiority.

Watching X-rated movies became cool and fun — as long as I ultimately condemned them. I loved talking about how bad the videos were, pointing out the pimples on performers' asses and mimicking the orgasmic fakery of the starlets. Criticizing pornography made me feel high and mighty both as a wannabe filmmaker and a human being, and it was so easy to do.

But admitting to myself that some of it was, finally, beginning to turn me on was not so easy. Sometimes I'd watch a woman on all fours beg for cock and think, *How humiliating.* Other times I'd watch the same sexual act in a different movie and instantly get wet, without stopping to analyze. I couldn't explain what flipped the switch. All I knew was that some of the very images I once defined as "male-oriented" and "inherently degrading" were now sexually exciting to me. Pornography, I realized, could be stupid, depressing and incredibly arousing.

But I wasn't having what Greg was having. I didn't feel the kind of connection with this stuff that would induce me to fill up my closet with it. Certain scenes turned me on, but then my arousal faded as quickly as it appeared. Watching him watch the screen, I got aroused when he got aroused. But this vicarious eroticism worried me. When he slipped into the funhouse, I stood outside, waiting.

I didn't understand the appeal of porn until the day I stopped looking for a political theory and let myself go. I made an important decision to be alone with pornography; to watch it without peer pressure, without talking. I made a date with an all-lesbian video titled *Aerobisex Girls.* It was rated four stars in *Adult Video News* because of its novel ten-woman oil-orgy scene. (Greg almost exclusively rented "all-lesbian action," and I soon grew fond of the genre myself.) I was determined not to care about the plot. I didn't wonder about the performers' family histories. I was determined not to think about anything except what my body was feeling. I started off by fingering myself in sync with the women in the film. I opened and closed my eyes, first imagining I was a voyeur and then a player in their scene. I grabbed the remote and rewound the shots I liked. I mentally cut back and forth between the images on the TV screen and my favorite close-ups I had stored in my memory, splicing together an erotic sequence that played only in my head. When I came, it was intense.

It was next to impossible for me to keep my epiphany to myself. I began leaking it in the most hushed tones to a few select ears, mostly other students, the ones whose films about shooting heroin involved close-ups of needles going into veins and other, you know, *transgressive* imagery. I expected people to be shocked, intrigued, perhaps even fall over laughing. But I was totally unprepared for indifference. More often than not, when I'd tell a man about my pornographic revelation, he'd give me the blankest of blank looks and say something like, "So you beat off to some porn. Big deal. I did that when I was thirteen."

Yeah, well I didn't masturbate until I was nearly twenty years old and a vibrator clocked me. A twenty-year-old guy who doesn't masturbate until an appliance hits him on the head is unimaginable. I never met a man who didn't know where his penis was or what it was for. (Conversely, I never met a woman who came too soon.) Once I figured out how to use porn and come — how to look at an erotic image and use my sexual imagination to turn desire into a self-generated orgasm — my life was irrevocably and positively changed. Now I understood the power of sexual fantasy and realized that my own sexual satisfaction was a state of mind that existed independently from a lover's touch or the perfect romantic moment.

Before my rendezvous with *Aerobisex Girls,* I didn't even know what a sexual fantasy was; I hadn't really had any. When I masturbated I only thought about the physical sensations. When I had sex with another person my thoughts were filled only with them, the way they were touching me, the immediacy of the act. And that was good. But pornography made me aware the sexual imagination isn't limited to the heat of the moment or a sensual reminiscence. I could think about *anything.* I could use *anything* for erotic inspiration. For the first time in my life, I felt sexually autonomous.

• • •

I began taking trips to the adult video section by myself. Beyond the swinging doors or gauzy curtains, the scene was pretty tense. Men with their eyes straight ahead, not saying a word. Either my timing was impeccable or my presence irked them, because one by one, they'd quickly disappear until I had the entire section to myself.

I wanted videos that, for starters, had plots with a psychological edge. All the happy-go-lucky fucking and sucking was getting tiresome. I wanted a story with conflict, with sexual tension between the characters; a story that poked around in the pornographic goo of the subconscious. But these kinds of films were a thing of the past. Much of the big-budget porn films of the 1970s and early '80s did feature disturbing, psychosexual dramatizations. Taking their cues from Hollywood, X-rated movies incorporated all the themes used in any box-office thriller — rape, incest, drug-trafficking, murder — and then added explicit sex. (When '70s anti-porn feminists insisted that pornography was violent, these are the types of films they pointed to.) With the advent of the Meese Commission, however, and their claim that pornography caused violent behavior, the FBI began cracking down on porn producers and distributors. After many successful prosecutions, the adult industry decided to play it safe and eliminated the most controversial elements, leaving us with the mostly bland offerings we have today.

I also wanted good-looking men who weren't afraid to touch other men, women who didn't look like Malibu Barbie and, most important, authentic female orgasms. Yet video after video was filled with the most stupid and contrived notions of what women do when they get horny. One tape showed a woman pretending to masturbate with a big pointy seashell. In another, a nude woman donned elbow-length gloves then ran out into the garden and started humping an oak tree. Here's a classic: two femmes in a haystack wearing white anklets, stiletto heels and floppy denim hats who stick out their tongues and pretend to French each other? Not in a million years, pal.

I also wanted camaraderie. I felt so isolated, as if I was the only woman in the world having positive experiences with pornography. I hadn't heard of "women's erotica" or "feminist pornography" because the genres barely existed back then. And I was scared to tell Sooze about my conversion, especially since talking to each other had become such a drag. The humor we once intuitively shared had vanished. She quit drinking, became a vegetarian and started buying records by lesbian folksingers. I stayed out all night, wore only black and worked on perfecting my sense of self-importance. I hated her stupid girlfriend and she hated my stupid boyfriend. The last straw was only a matter of time.

I found solace in my local bookstore, which had a handful of sex books by women, and I bought them all: Lonnie Barbach's gentle erotic anthologies, *Pleasures* and *Erotic Interludes;* Nancy Friday's *My Secret Garden* and *Forbidden Flowers,* collections of women's sexual fantasies; Erica Jong's *Fear of Flying* and the classics by Anaïs Nin. (I passed on Pauline Réage's S/M novel, *The Story of O,* because I believed the rumor that it was written by a man.) I scanned magazines, newspapers and underground zines looking for any mention of female artists who might be doing something sexually relevant, which is how I uncovered Candida Royalle's series of feminist adult videos, the work of photographer Annie Sprinkle and *On Our Backs,* a magazine billed as "Entertainment for the Adventurous Lesbian," edited by Susie Bright. Pornography created by women for women struck me as absolutely revolutionary because it challenged the myth that women are not — and should not be — interested in erotic pictures.

No other source articulated this challenge more incisively for me than *Caught Looking.* Published by FACT (the Feminist Anti-Censorship Taskforce), this magazine-style anthology combined academic refutations of the anti-porn argument with sexually explicit pictures. As its title implies, it gave women the rare opportunity to look at a wide variety of pornographic images from the 1890s to the 1980s. All of the essays presented the case that censorship of sexual expression was not only unconstitutional but unfeminist.

Feminism is not now and never has been in agreement on how best to advance women's sexual independence. Since the so-called first wave of feminism in the nineteenth century, many feminists defined female sexuality as intrinsically soft, nurturing and pure, therefore in need of *more* legal protection to keep it safe from men's intrinsically predatory, totalitarian and violent sexuality. But other feminists believed that women needed *less* protection in order to take greater control of their bodies, their sexuality and their lives. When pornography became a central issue in the twentieth century, the movement was still divided. Many feminists felt that restricting women's access to sexual speech and censoring sexually "deviant" imagery in the name of protecting women signaled more oppression, not liberation. Yet the question remained: How to eliminate egregious sexism and violence against women and still support freedom of erotic expression?

My answer was to try to create nonsexist pornography. Spurred on by my own experiences, I began work on a two-page zine called *Magnet School: A Sexographic Magazine* under the pen name Lisa LaBia. I thought my pseudonym was catchy and fun, and it turned out to be educational as well, because there were plenty of people who simply thought I was Italian. I hammered out the first issue on my typewriter, reprinting text from a Throwing Muses album, daring a girlfriend to pen a porn story and pirating some hard-core images I liked from some magazines. I photocopied it for free in the middle of the night at the twenty-four-hour copy place, since I'd made friends with the anarchist punks who worked there. I handed it out in cafés and bars, and made rounds to every dirty bookstore in town, telling every dildo clerk about the coming of the next erotic revolution. It was very grass-roots.

In the battle against pornography, the words *degrading* and *oppressive* were presented as absolute, objective terms. Yet I found them to be vague and subjective, especially when I asked myself the following questions: Is the very act of a woman spreading her legs and wanting sex degrading? Are photographs of her genitals oppressive? Why is this image of female desire consistently read as exploitative rather than powerful and liberating? Furthermore, if we're going to examine degrading images of women, why limit ourselves to pornography? What about, say, laundry soap commercials and their depiction of women whose self-worth revolves around removing stains?

To me, the biggest problem with porn was its artificiality and predictability. I wanted to create something that aroused people sexually and intellectually, that dealt with the complexity — and humor — of human sexuality. Because I so badly wanted to produce something different, I called it something different: sexography. There were other contenders for the title — cliterature, lustography, climaxerox — but they didn't have the right ring. (Calling it sexography was also a convenient way for me to duck out of the erotica vs. pornography debate.) In Issue One, I defined sexography as "absolutely no writing about harlots, no getting off with big orchids, no high heels in bed, no split beavers and no masturbating to Lionel Ritchie." That definition is so silly to me now, but it exemplifies an inclination among almost all of us to separate the "right" kind of sex from the "wrong," to discern nice pictures from dirty ones, to draw the line.

Although I'd told myself I could use anything for erotic inspiration — I didn't. I couldn't shake the belief that certain sexual fantasies should be off-limits, that there were certain scenarios I should never, ever attach sexual feelings to. I was stuck on the idea that feminists were supposed to have certain kinds of cheerful, egalitarian fantasies, even though I rarely had them myself.

• • •

I made my first visit to San Francisco in 1986. High on my list of sights to see was a women's sex toy store I'd heard about called Good Vibrations. At the time it was just a tiny storefront in the Mission District. Now it's a multimillion-dollar business. Unlike the adult bookstores I'd been in, this place was sunny and smelled good, and the sales clerk was actually helpful. The selection was limited: vibrators and some books. But they had one book I never saw in the stores back home: *Coming to Power: Writings and Graphics on Lesbian S/M,* the title boldly spelled out in giant red letters. Great for my collection, I thought. It was an anthology of erotic fiction and essays put out by a lesbian leather group called Samois, on the politics of sadomasochism. I couldn't wait to read it on the plane back to the Twin Cities.

Stuck in a middle seat, I pretended not to notice the alternately horrified and inquisitive looks I was getting from the guys in suits on either side of me. *Are they going to ask me to put it away? Or ask me if I'm "into" leather?*

When I got to the story called "Girl Gang" by Crystal Bailey, however, I had to put the book away anyway because it was the most politically incorrect thing I'd ever read and it was turning me on so much I couldn't stand it. In it, a dominant lesbian butch meets Benta, a tough gorgeous submissive femme. By the second page, Benta is in the backroom of a leather bar on her knees, obeying orders to eat pussy from a whole gang of women and not wearing much more than the collar and leather thong that ties her wrists behind her back. After Benta endures endless erotic teasing, the butch asks,

> "You ever heard of a gang bang, Benta?"
> "Yes." She lowered her eyes. We could hear her swallow in the tense silence of the room.
> "You want to get fucked like that, Benta?"
> "Yes, yes, yes."

Benta gets everything: tied up, whipped, fingered, fucked with the whip handle, slapped in the face, clamps put on her nipples. She ends up having a couple of great big orgasms, and when it's all over she is worshiped with kisses by everyone.

My guilty conscience arrived right on time, whispering, That's *bad*. How could any woman want such things?

I wanted so badly to be Benta.

I was reminded of the time when I was seven or so, and I endured a boring visit to my uncle's house by sitting too close to the TV and changing channels. I stopped when I saw a muscled-up prisoner kneeling down, hands tied behind his back, shirt off in the hot sun in a jungle somewhere. An enemy leader was whipping the prisoner, trying to get information out of him, but he wouldn't give it up. Instantly I got hit by an all-over tingly crazy feeling. The scene got me so worked up that afterward I gnawed on my uncle's hi-fi and left two giant front-tooth marks on it, which got me in a whole lot of trouble. I felt bad for liking this scene — but not bad enough. I tracked down this show in *TV Guide*, but none of the subsequent episodes featured another whipping scene or anything even close. For years after, whenever I had trouble falling asleep, I'd think about the prisoner taking a beating. Imagining the cruelty gave me a soothing, warm feeling that rocked me to sleep. I knew it was a naughty thing to think. And I knew thinking about it felt good.

After my trip to the West Coast, I decided to break the ice and show the book to Sooze. I figured that since it was written by real San Francisco lesbians, we might find some common ground. She'd read it. In fact, she was writing an anti-S/M term paper that argued that S/M is violence against women and used the book as evidence. I, on the other hand, was making a film inspired by my own small explorations into S/M.

"Why would a woman want to wear clothespins on her nipples and be in pain? That is a fucked-up male invention," she said.

"It's not like you wear them to the grocery store. You have to be in a scene, you have to be turned on," I replied.

The collapse of our friendship was now complete.

Of course, Sooze wasn't the first person to have a problem with S/M. Historically, sex researchers from Freud to Masters and Johnson have viewed most sexual practices outside the missionary position as either pathologies to be cured or bad behaviors to be unlearned. The most bizarre example of this is Richard von Krafft-Ebing's horrifying opus *Psychopathia Sexualis,* written in 1886, where sexual desire is presented as a festering pit of abnormality that provokes gruesome acts of homosexuality, masturbation, murder and dismemberment. A classic advertisement for the book reads: "Startling case histories of unnatural sex practices, weird auto-erotic methods, sex — lust — torture — and much, much more! . . . Monstrous, strange, almost unbelievable sex acts!" It's laughable, except that its fictions had such a chilling impact. Homosexuality was listed as a pathology in the Diagnostic and Statistical Manual until the early 1970s. The practices of sadism and masochism still are, with no distinction between a serial killer like Jeffrey Dahmer and a caring professional like Mistress Kat.

Although it would be years until I tried on a clothespin, the psychology of erotic dominance and submission immediately drew me in. Still, I couldn't help wondering why I got turned on by the things that seem to be the antithesis of love, like pain and humiliation. Warm fuzzy fantasies about making love weren't the only ones that made me come. It seemed risky to me, to play in the dark with these particular feelings. It still does.

...

My senior thesis at the Minneapolis College of Art and Design was a 16mm film titled *What You Want*. I described it as a dark and abstract narrative that dealt with issues of female sexuality, power and eroticism. Basically it was the thinly veiled story of my life, starring me in a long red wig since no one else auditioned. Greg played The Boyfriend. The script called for us to get naked in a bathtub together and have (simulated) oral sex, and for me to (fake) pierce his nipple, fuck with his mind and then leave him in the dust. During student critiques, everyone was very lively and opinionated until I showed my work-in-progress. Dead silence was followed by "What are your parents going to think?" I successfully managed to ignore that anxiety-provoking question until the day of my college graduation.

My father had been surprisingly supportive when I first announced my decision to become a filmmaker, since he was once an aspiring *auteur* himself. His masterpiece was an 8mm short about the day I was born, titled *The Pitter Patter of Little Feet.* It opened with my mother sitting at the kitchen table, in labor, motioning to my father to get his damn camera out of her face. Next, a close-up of hands on a clock whizzing around and around. At 6:31 cut to: an out-of-focus shot of twinkling glass beads that slowly revolve, as a metaphor for the moment of my birth. It was very Hays Code.

During my senior year I frequently wrote letters to my father describing the subject of my film in the most unspecific half-truths — my favorite words being *abstract, dark* and *narrative* — then asking for money to finish it. He always replied with one of his trademark instructions for victory — "Pull yourself up by your bootstraps!" — and enclosed a check signed with love. He was truly happy that I had found my calling and was actively pursuing it.

On graduation day, however, my father was incensed because I had refused to make a fancy dinner reservation after the commencement. I insisted that we all stick around for the party and film screenings at the school instead. It was *my* graduation, and I was going to celebrate it *my* way. This seemingly small break with tradition was, in fact, big enough to send fountains of family bullshit flying every which way.

After I received my diploma, I took a few perfunctory photos with my parents, siblings and their respective spouses and then we joined the party, where my father continued to make a big show of his displeasure. The rest of us shifted our weight from one uncomfortable foot to the other, inspected the ice in our glasses and tried to act casual while we waited for the next bomb to explode. I thought the screening would be a relief, because for the next hour or so, none of us would have to speak.

My work appeared about halfway through the program. First, I showed a video of home movies juxtaposed with images of urban decay set to a Kate Bush tune. It elicited many loud and insightful comments from my mother, such as "Oh, look! There's Lisa as a baby wearing my babushka!" and "I looked so young back then!"

Finally, the feature presentation. The film opened with me pretending to chain-smoke while I talked about sex. Things began rocketing floorward when people laughed out loud at what I considered to be the most meaningful and erotically provocative dialogue of my film and began whispering, "This is so *bad!*" Out of the corner of my eye, I glanced down the row at my father. He was baring his teeth. *Oh no. Oh God. Why didn't I just become a nurse?* On the big screen, Greg and I were naked in the bathtub. Now my head was moving slowly down Greg's chest, down, down, to his nether-regions. I wanted to stand up and scream, "STOP this insanity! Rewind! Everyone, forget what you just saw!" And I would have done it, too, except at that very moment, as if directed by my own telekinetic powers, the film got jammed in the projector and snapped. The screen went white, and then the theater went dark. My father walked out.

I took off after him, through the lobby and out into the street. He was walking superfast, not saying a word. I ran along behind him crying, apologizing and saying anything I thought might quell his anger, including the ridiculous "You were right! Let's have dinner." Then he stopped and turned around. His face was blank but his eyes were raging with contempt.

"I can't believe I wasted thirty thousand dollars on your education. You'll never amount to shit."

Our opinions about each other escalated into an abusive screaming match on the sidewalk as other, happier graduates and their parents walked around us. My mother caught up to us, shrieking, "I can't believe this is happening!" My brothers calmly tried to intervene, all the while holding their hands up in case any punches accidentally came their way. In the midst of it all, a car full of teenage boys drove by honking and whistling and ultimately shouting, "Woo-hoo! Nice rack!" in response to my form-fitting dress. That was it. "Fuuuuuck yooouuuu!" I'd never gone absolutely berserk in public before. It was a terrible sensation but I couldn't stop. "Fuck you fuck you fuck you ALL!" I screamed, until I collapsed on the sidewalk. A college friend, who had watched the madness unfold, rushed in and offered to take me home.

My father and I didn't speak to each other after that. I wrote him a long, well-intentioned but harsh letter, the gist of which was that fatherhood is about more than accidents of biology and footing the bills, and that he needed to take responsibility for all of his hurtful actions if he wanted my love. He never responded. Eight months later, he died of a heart attack in his sleep.

The day of his death I drove home to Chicago, the road barely visible through my tears. Preparing for his funeral was, surprisingly, a tremendous distraction from my grief. There was a lot to do: choose a casket, pick the pallbearers, select Dad's eternal outfit. My mother asked me to go to the basement, where my father kept all of his clothes, and polish his shoes. As I poked around looking for the shoeshine kit, I came across a pad of paper, sitting atop a messy pile of receipts and financial statements. The first six or seven pages each read, "Dear Lisa . . ." and contained the beginnings of a letter, which was then scribbled out in an effort to get it just right. The sentences were all slightly different but the sentiment was the same: *Please forgive me for all of my failures as a father. I never wanted to hurt you. I love you more than life itself.*

• • •

They say the truth will set you free, but they forget to tell you not everyone will celebrate your freedom.

I always knew the subject of sex, with its age-old reputation of being dirty, shameful and bad was a loaded one. That's what attracted me to it. Artists are supposed to look into the heart of darkness and embrace dissent, not win popularity contests. I assumed my adversaries would be nameless strangers in a talk-show audience, or some know-it-all critics or possibly even feminists "out there" who just didn't get it. Instead I was rejected by the people I loved the most and it was devastating.

At its core feminism is the belief in every woman's right to determine her own truth. But what was *my* truth? Why was I compelled to explore a subject that made everyone so uncomfortable? There was no shortage of opinions: I'm acting out. Getting back at my parents. Into shock value. Rebelling. True, I once defined myself by rebellion. But now I defined myself by my accomplishments, my relationships with other people and with myself. I *cared* what people thought and, secretly, even a look of disapproval felt like a punch in the guts. Yet it wasn't enough to stop me. I couldn't shake the feeling that I was being pulled down some dimly lit corridor, toward a glowing lump of knowledge I wasn't even sure I wanted.

3

Girl Pornographer

I'D ALWAYS ASSUMED MY sex-positive activism was just a phase that would end when I got a real job — or wrote my million-dollar screenplay and landed a director's chair with my name on it. Then I got fifty bucks for my first erotic short story and began rethinking my options.

Originally, I wrote "Jane's Train" for myself and published it in *Magnet School*. After reading so much erotica I thought, as many do, *I could do better than that!* and started typing. The story is about a young woman who uses her feelings of sexual jealousy to fuel a hot masturbatory fantasy. Like so many pieces of fiction, this one was also based on the author's personal experience. Greg and I had decided to take a stab at an open relationship, at being nonmonogamous. Two problems surfaced immediately: One, he was getting lots of action and I got zero. Two, he paraded his trophies right in front of me. When I saw him making out with Girl #2 I remained cool on the outside, but inside I was furious. I felt the best mature, adult way to expel my jealousy was to offer it eternal life in print. The other was to take Greg up on his offer that I "see other people, have new adventures." A few weeks later, the following conversation took place:

Me: You know that guy Phil I've been seeing?
Greg: Yeah.
Me: We moved in together yesterday, so I'm breaking up with you.

Phil was a dark-haired English-born poet-singer-songwriter heavily influenced by Leonard Cohen and Bob Dylan. He was also an excellent cook, an accomplished stained-glass artist and the first man I ever lived with. He read me poems like "Ode on a Grecian Urn" and bits from William Blake's "The Marriage of Heaven and Hell," and explained each line to me. It was all very romantic except for his inability to keep his guitar in tune, which resulted in countless off-key renditions of "Tangled Up in Blue."

We took off on a year-long trip to Europe, and upon my return I received a form letter from a company called Down There Press seeking submissions for an anthology of women's erotica. In 1988, "Jane's Train" was published in *Herotica,* edited by San Francisco sex writer Susie Bright.

I was overjoyed at being published, but I still had no idea of how to make a living as a writer. Or a filmmaker for that matter. So I took a job working at Dayton's department store in their Christmas ornament section, and on Christmas day, at age twenty-five, I woke up with chicken pox, no doubt contracted from one of the hundreds of runny-nosed kids who crashed into the display of blinking Italian lights and gold cherubs on their way to sit in Santa's lap. Next, I worked as a receptionist at KQRS, a classic rock station, where the indisputable highlight was "A Cruise with the Nuge," a promotion where fifty listeners called in to win a three-hour boat ride down the St. Croix river with Ted Nugent. Unfortunately it was raining on the big day and so we were all trapped inside the small cabin with Ted, while he cranked up his guitar amp to eleven for the extended instrumental versions of "Wang Dang Sweet Poontang" and other favorites.

The question remained: What am I going to do with my life? One evening, I worked up the courage to call Susie Bright long-distance from Minnesota to thank her for publishing my piece. I'd never spoken to a real, live editor before. We talked for nearly three hours about sex, pornography, publishing, hair, makeup, celebrities, love relationships and the rest of our lives.

"When I was sixteen I was a member of this socialist group called the Red Tide," Susie confided, "and I would break down and cry all the time because I wasn't alive during the Bolshevik revolution to fight the fight and hang out with Lenin. No. I was forced to be a seventies teenager living in Los Angeles."

"Oh, I know exactly what you mean. As a child I used to have terrible crying fits because Sonny and Cher weren't my parents."

Susie invited me out for a visit to San Francisco for a week, and I jumped. When she picked me up at the airport, though, I was a bit disappointed. She didn't *look* like Susie Sexpert. She looked like a goody-goody fifties teenager in her horn-rimmed glasses, bouncy brown ponytail and capri pants. A clever disguise. "Hi there," she said in a voice so full of sugar I half-expected her next words to be "Come here often?" Then she reached for the huge suitcase I was dragging like a dead cow and effortlessly whisked it away with a single hand. She stood nearly six feet tall in her blue Keds and I had to walk-walk-run just to keep up with her on the way to her "secret" parking spot in the airport garage, which involved a perilous jaywalk through the "Return to Terminal" speedway. She drove a red Toyota MR2 — license plate Too2Big — and floored it all the way to her Bernal Heights apartment.

"Change your clothes, because we're going to a party." Susie yanked open the double doors to her closet and I was blinded by the brilliance of its contents. There were sequins, satins, polka dots, leopard prints, gold lamé, skimpy black leather items with silver chains and a puzzling amount of tie-dye. At least fifty pairs of size 11 high-heeled pumps lined the closet floor. A full-length, crimson velvet cape and a white tutu whizzed past me and landed on the bed. Drawers flew open, full of silk lingerie and latex accessories I didn't even know existed. A rhinestone tiara and a marabou boa were briefly examined and then tossed aside. I felt as if I were watching the transformation of a superhero from inside the phone booth.

An entire wall of Susie's bedroom was devoted to jewelry, mainly earrings, attached to long pieces of black velvet. Another wall of windows faced west out over the hilly expanse of the city and Twin Peaks. The fog was rolling in, the last of the sunset colored the room and the moment was incredibly cinematic. I sat on her bed consumed with awe — and despair. Everything in my suitcase was so wrong, so pedestrian! I didn't even own a pair of high heels. "Is it okay if I just wear this?" I said quietly, glancing down at my black T-shirt, jeans and army boots. I figured it was better to be completely understated than try to compete. Susie lifted my chin with a soft hand.

"Cinderella, do you need something to wear to the ball?" I nodded like a pouty two-year-old who is finally given some attention.

The book release party for Steve Chapple and David Talbot's *Burning Desires: Sex in America* was held in a funky club South of Market where fashion knew no rules. But when Susie walked in, people literally stepped back. Not only did the plunging neckline of her minidress boldly showcase her gravity-defying 38C breasts but the skirt was like a giant orange parking cone, and its sheer diameter created an aisle for Susie wherever she went. I trailed along behind her, feeling marvelous in an off-the-shoulder, one-size-fits-all tourquoise and purple Lycra sheath.

The evening's entertainment included a video screening of actor Rob Lowe having sex in a hotel room, and a live striptease by Nina Hartley. I'd read all about Nina's background — red diaper baby raised in Berkeley who grew up to be a nurse, radical feminist and successful porn star — and I couldn't wait to meet her that night. But I got more than I bargained for when Nina flung her G-string into the crowd, and Susie caught it.

When we got home we raced down the hall into Susie's bedroom, giggling and pinching each other the whole way.

"You go first!"

"No you!"

We couldn't wait to take turns trying on our little prize in front of the mirror, doing our best Nina Hartley poses and giving each other lewd directions.

"Worship my perfect ass, you bastards!"

"Wait! My camera!"

"How does Nina stand it with this tiny string going up her butt crack?"

We were carrying on at the top of our lungs and snapping pictures when the door to Susie's bedroom burst open and this butch dyke in a black leather jacket and an English accent shouted, "WHAT THE FUCK IS GOING ON?"

For a split-second, time stopped. Susie was nude except for black high heels, her eyebrows raised, mouth frozen in the O of surprise, hands primly clasped together. Jill Posener, Susie's housemate, stood in the doorway snarling, one hand crushing the doorknob, the other in midair, all five fingers splayed. I was completely unclothed, holding the G-string in my hand, a biblical quotation stuck in my head: *I heard the sound of thee in the garden, and I was afraid because I was naked.* That old sick feeling of being caught with my pants down was all over me and I was convinced that whatever the problem was, my nude frolicking was the cause.

"WHY ARE THE CATS OUT IN THE MIDDLE OF THE STREET?" Jill continued. Time lurched forward. Susie shot back with a furious commentary on the condition of the front door and how it wasn't her fault if it didn't lock and the cats escaped. While they argued, I waited patiently for my turn to be yelled at for being naked. But I soon realized that if I wanted to be guilty and ashamed, I was going to have to feel it all by myself because neither Jill nor Susie gave a rat's ass about me and my nudism. I was naked — naked! — and nobody cared.

The next morning over breakfast, Susie, her mouth stuffed with toast, says, "What do you say we get pierced?" I start to tell her I already got my ears pierced, when she cuts me off. "I'm talking about your pussy — a labia ring." She swallows.

"It's totally the latest thing. I've been thinking about doing it for months but," her voice sinks to a whisper, "I'm too scared to go alone!"

A few hours later I'm in Oakland sitting with my legs spread over the arms of an overstuffed chair, wide open to experience. There is a small ink dot on my right inner labium to mark the spot where a small gold ring is going to go. Raelyn Gallina, an expert piercer with serious tattoos up and down her arms and eight holes in the ear I can see, is holding a large needle in her surgically gloved hand. "On the count of three I'm going to stick it through, "she says.

"I can't believe you want to go first." Susie is cringing with anticipation. "You're so brave!"

"I'm not brave, I'm selfish," I say, trying not to hyperventilate. "I cut to the front because I couldn't bear to hear your screams knowing I was next."

Surprisingly, it was the metaphysics of the experience, not the pain, that sent me reeling. After what was (honest!) a two-second sting, I was floating somewhere above the natural world in a calm, transcendent state that lasted for hours. I also felt indescribably feminine, as if that needle had pushed me into womanhood in a way that losing my virginity never did.

My consciousness continued to rise well into the next morning, when Jill Posener asked me quite matter-of-factly, "So, how's your cunt?" It was the first time I had ever heard anyone say this word without anger, without the slightest hint of eroticism or embarrassment. It stopped me in my tracks. "My . . . cunt," I said slowly, trying out my new word, "is doing just fine." There. Said it.

The rest of the week was filled with equally memorable firsts, including landing my first magazine job. Before I left,

Susie offered me an editorial position at *On Our Backs,* the lesbian sex magazine she edited, and I accepted. I returned home and told my boyfriend Phil, rather indelicately, that I was going to San Francisco without him. He helped me get there just a little bit faster by throwing all of my shit out on the front porch. He wasn't the only one who wanted to know: Did you fuck Susie Bright? Are you a big lesbian now?

The answers were, respectively, no and no. Our relationship has never been predicated on getting in each other's pants or on my induction into the lesbian nation. That we shared the same convictions was obvious the minute we met. There was no subject too unspeakable, no joke too sick, no tears too foolish. Instantly, we were soulmates, confidants, partners in crime. And the day Susie grabbed my hand and we leapt into the chaos called San Francisco, it was like Butch Cassidy and the Sundance Kid jumping off that cliff. Only for us, it was just the beginning.

· · ·

The day I headed out west was a scene not unlike *The Beverly Hillbillies.* I bought a rusted-out 1978 Ford F150 for $200 and loaded up the truck. To me, San Francisco was a mad sex carnival where anything seemed possible. The home of Miss Carol Doda, America's first topless dancer, who was lowered into the audience on a piano that came out of the ceiling; of Haight-Ashbury love-ins, porn emporiums, queer culture, safe-sex parties, the pierced-and-tattooed scene.

Ever since the Gold Rush, when people had money to burn and a remote peninsula on which to burn it, San Francisco has lived up to its wild reputation as the sexual frontier. In

1970, city supervisor Dianne Feinstein (who later became mayor, then senator) disgustedly observed, "We have become a kind of smut capital of the United States." Well, it didn't get that way because there was something in the water. The hows and whys of San Francisco's sexual history are a complex archaeological dig, and lots of things combined to make The City an atmosphere ripe for revolution — new technology, a stable economy, national political turbulence, local social tolerance and breathtaking geographic beauty that attracted all kinds. But the notorious porn explosion of the 1960s and early 1970s was also tied to the legal definition of obscenity. In 1957 the Supreme Court (in *United States* v. *Roth*) redefined obscenity as material "*utterly* without redeeming social importance" and (unintentionally) opened the floodgates for sexual expression. As long as the teensiest speck of "social importance" could be extracted from even the most sexually explicit stuff, well, that was enough to squeeze on through. Especially in San Francisco.

Of course, San Francisco is famous for many things besides sex. Like earthquakes. On October 17, 1989, just two weeks after my arrival, with the entire country tuned to the World Series at Candlestick Park, The City was hit by a fifteen-second earthquake that measured 7.1 on the Richter scale. It was like bad airplane turbulence except I was on the ground. Streets split open, buildings were leveled, fires broke out, freeways collapsed, the Bay Bridge came apart, power was out, phones were down. Hey, welcome to town.

The *On Our Backs* office, which had been spared destruction, was located above a stinky Chinese restaurant in the openly gay Castro district, where women walked down the street kissing and holding hands and mustachioed leather daddies walked around in nothing but nipple clamps and chaps. Founded in 1984 by publishers Debi Sundahl, Nan Kinney and editor Susie Bright, *On Our Backs* was a small-budget, black-and-white publication with a big mission: to blatantly show and tell everything about lesbian sexuality that the party-line feminist press refused to. (The very title was a play on the women's newspaper of "correct" sexual politics, *Off Our Backs*, although not everyone got it. My mother wasn't the only one who sent me mail addressed to *On Your Backs*, as if to say, *You* may be on *your* back, but not me.) Each issue was filled with articles like "James Dean: The Almost Perfect Lesbian Hermaphrodite," "The Dildo Crisis," "What Do Butches Want in Bed?" and "How to Read a Dirty Movie." But it was the pictures that fanned the flames of controversy. Fat motorcycle dykes in strap-ons gang-banging a dreadlocked blonde; a smiling coed with a Barbie doll shoved feet-first up her hairy coochie; a queer army reservist — who'd been dishonorably discharged during Operation Desert Storm — with her fatigues around her ankles, fingering herself in the sand. There were also lots of traditional soft-core nudes, but it was the explicit photos of radical sex that stirred things up.

My first day as assistant editor I was skimming through some back issues and came across one of Susie's how-to editorials, titled "A Hand in the Bush." It opens with the sentence "One of the great misunderstood characters of the world is the lesbian fistfucker." I'll say. They were so misunderstood I hadn't even heard of them. Truthfully, I didn't know if I wanted to — the idea of someone sticking her whole hand in my cunt! Instinctively I crossed my legs. *Who am I kidding? I am in way over my head.*

Quickly, I tried to calm myself with this thought: If fistfucking *didn't* strike me as weird, it would surely be a sign that I was sliding down the slippery slope of depravity. That one day there would be absolutely nothing I found disturbing about sex — or about anything! My own sexual morality would have decomposed so slowly I wouldn't even notice until it was gone and I would be saying things like "Nothing's shocking" and "Anything goes."

It wasn't the first time — or the last — I felt this ping-pong of emotions: grossed out by some sexual act, ashamed of my uptight response, but worried that feeling nothing would be even worse. Back when I was doing *Magnet School,* fellow travelers Annie Sprinkle and Veronica Vera sent me a copy of *Love* magazine, a reader-written, sexually explicit journal, where I came across some self-portraits of Fakir Musafar, the now-famous godfather of the modern primitive movement. At first I couldn't tell what was going on in the photos. In one, it looked like he had a thick steel bar stuck to his bare chest. Then I realized the bar was going through both of his nipples. On the facing page he was nude, suspended by giant metal hooks through his chest, and there were weights hanging from his balls. *Why would anybody want to do that?*

The text, which was at times funny, described his manipulations as a quest for transcendence. He said he was seeking "an experience" even if it meant death. What he achieved was a kind of hallucinatory out-of-body experience that left him feeling very calm and post-orgasmic. I felt sick and slammed the magazine shut, wishing I'd never seen it.

Part of me thought, *See? This is what happens on the road to sexual liberation. You start out wanting an orgasm and pretty soon you're hanging by your tits from a meathook to get one.* Another part thought, *One day I'm going to wake up and find myself standing out in front of Woolworth's shouting Scripture into a megaphone and wearing a plywood board that reads, "Whores of Babylon, repent!" and all my friends will shake their heads and say, "She used to be such a freethinker."* I feared that steady exposure to sexual words and images would make the delicate rubber bands that held my personality together snap, and I'd go shooting off in some extreme direction, becoming either an insatiable sex maniac or a religious nutcase. My lingering fear of getting The Calling wasn't as crazy as it sounds — if it happened to Larry Flynt, it could happen to me! (*Hustler* publisher Larry Flynt saw the light thanks to then-president Jimmy Carter's sister and became a born-again Christian just before the infamous Meat Grinder issue hit the stands.) Or maybe I'd simply go numb. I mean, once I've seen it all, then what? Will I do anything for an erotic kick? Worse, will I become indifferent to the pain and suffering of humanity?

These questions weren't miles away, floating out in the stratosphere of Life's Big Mysteries — they were in my face. After all, my shock tolerance had increased significantly in just a few short years. Images that once shocked me — extreme bondage, facial come shots — now barely registered. I did sexual things I never thought I would do — like getting my labia pierced, for one — and liked them. But where did I draw the line? Would I reach a point where every single sexual practice between consenting adults was perfectly acceptable to me? The idea was frightening. When pornography became the currency of my profession, however, I had to confront this fear and risk finding out exactly what would happen when I immersed myself in a vat of sex.

Working at *On Our Backs* was, in so many respects, like

working at any magazine. I assigned, edited and wrote copy on deadline. I took minutes at our weekly editorial meetings where our nine-woman staff sat around (A) listening to the publisher — who really wanted to be the editor — decide which of her personal problems she should answer in her self-penned advice column; (B) pissing about why some of our contributors never managed to hand in their work on time; and (C) deciding if we'd even be able to go to press since we hadn't paid the last print bill. The main difference was that every day at *On Our Backs* I talked about sex and looked at pictures of people having sex and met with people — nice, wholesome people! — who shared their personal, sexual insights with me. Subsequently, sex lost much of its taboo quality and, over time, took on a much more balanced — though no less interesting — shape, and being "shocked by sex" was no longer an accurate gauge for my own morality.

One of the ongoing topics of office conversation was What's the difference between erotica and pornography? We talked about the cultural tendency to define *erotica* as tender, loving and romantic while *pornography* is raw, loveless and crass. As in, Erotica = Good, Pornography = Bad. We considered the slightly more objective method of separating erotica from pornography by levels of explicitness. As in, if a woman has her legs closed, it's erotica; if they're spread, it's pornography. Intent is another illusory measuring stick. If it intends to turn you on and succeeds, it's erotic. If it fails, it's pornographic. Often I'd be yammering on and on, attempting to craft the perfect response to the question I once avoided, when Susie, exasperated, would look up from her copy of French *Vogue* and snap, "The main distinction between erotica and pornography is class, okay?"

It's true. The most explicit, extreme sexual act is labeled erotica — and socially acceptable — if it's presented in an artful, high-class way. Working at the magazine I met plenty of people who shoved something up their ass and photographed it, but so far Robert Mapplethorpe is the only one who's made it to the Whitney Museum. Why? His work was bought by wealthy patrons — it aspired to be art. But when a piece of work isn't about anything else but inciting desire, it's called pornography.

As a result, much of what is considered offensive about pornography has to do with image and interpretation, not the sexual acts themselves. Take a woman sucking a man's cock until he comes all over her face, for example. The act is not intrinsically offensive, but a picture of it, depending on how it's photographed, may or may not be. It can be presented in a very crass way, or it can be depicted as beautiful and sensuous. Still, there are plenty of otherwise open-minded people who insist this type of come shot is *inherently* degrading and offensive, no matter how artfully presented, because they refuse to believe there can be other interpretations.

• • •

It was through my job at *On Our Backs* that I got my first opportunity to work on an X-rated movie. Debi Sundahl, our publisher, who also ran Fatale Video, makers of erotic videos by and for women, was about to direct *Suburban Dykes,* filmed, appropriately, on location at her Marin County home.

At eight o'clock in the morning on the day of the shoot, I followed Debi and her trail of cigarette smoke through the foyer and into the kitchen. She was decked out in a tight black minidress and black boots that put her at about six feet, bright pink gloss on her lips and a healthy smear of silvery eyeshadow. I was wearing hi-tops and some wrinkled clothes I'd grabbed off my bedroom floor. *She didn't say anything about dressing up.* "Mitch is still asleep in the guest room," she called over her shoulder, referring to porn star Sharon Mitchell, "but everyone else is almost ready to go." Debi's giant blond hair formed an arc that went from elbow to elbow, and I watched it move in time with the swing of her ass.

Debi took a left into the living room and began making introductions, her heels sinking into the cream shag carpeting like it was sand. I said good morning to the all-female crew who were lugging gear and asking about coffee, and to one of the stars, Pepper, a long-haired Latina stripper with a fabulously crooked front tooth who'd been in a few other Fatale productions.

On the other side of the room, sitting on one of the overstuffed mauve leather sofas under a print of little duckies in silhouette, was superstar Nina Hartley. She wasn't in superstar mode, though. Flat hair, no makeup, glasses, wearing a T-shirt from some sunny vacation villa. You could bump into her in the produce aisle and never, ever guess what she did for a living. "This is our production assistant," Debi said, introducing me.

"I'm a big fan," I said, shaking Nina's hand, and neglecting to mention that I once partied with her G-string.

After I got the breakfast ready, we all assembled in a circle, paper plates on our laps, and started going over the script. The year: 1990. The setting: wealthy suburbia. The characters: Pepper, a butch, and Nina, a femme. The story: A yuppie lesbian couple decides to enhance their sex life by paying for phone sex, spying on two ham-thighed diesel dykes who get it on in the garage and hiring a lesbian escort. What made this film authentically lesbian was not only that it featured women having sex with each other and coming, but that it challenged the preconceptions that real lesbians don't like dildos, have kinky fantasies, fuck other butches or live in the sticks.

Nina grabbed a marker and began highlighting her lines. Rupa, the stylist, looked surprised and asked, "Is this the first time you've read the script?"

Nina nodded. "Most of the time I don't even get a script."

"So you're supposed to read the story, memorize your lines and act it all out *today?*" Rupa's jaw dropped.

"Of course she is!" cried Susie. "Don't you know the motto? Shot in a day, the porno way!"

Susie was hanging out on the set as team cheerleader and script doctor. In between shouting out dialogue suggestions and pithy slogans, I noticed Susie was shuffling through a box of papers, so I leaned over and asked her what she was doing.

"Organizing my taxes."

"Taxes? How can you possibly think about your *taxes* when people are going to be doing it right in front of you?"

"Look," she whispered, "I've been to these kinds of shoots before. It's hour after hour of standing around, waiting for the camera to roll. It drives me nuts. So this time I brought something to do while they're plugging in the star's vibrator."

"Ssshhhhh!" Debi hissed, glaring at the both of us.

I knew from experience that making movies was an excruciatingly slow start-and-stop process, where good takes are often separated by hours of dealing with technical problems, creative differences, flaky talent and uncontrollable forces of nature. Yet I couldn't help thinking because this was a *sex* film, I'd be so turned on the entire time the hours would fly by. Watching people have sex in person *had* to be better than watching them on video. *And pretty soon we'll all be dog-piling on each other because things will be so hot.* This last thought gave me a rush of anxiety. A group sex scene that I couldn't fast-forward or rewind? Where all of my sexual incompetence would be revealed? And while the idea of being attacked by lesbians was actually appealing, I didn't want them to be the lesbians I'd see the next day at the office.

By 2:00 P.M., however, there hadn't been a single sex scene and nobody made a pass at me. It was all very businesslike. We spent nearly three hours on the opening scene — Nina and Pepper Talking in Hot Tub — and we were setting up for Scene Two — Nina and Pepper Call Phone Sex — when I heard a piercing scream followed by "I can't take this anymore!" It was Mistress Marlayna, the phone sex dominatrix, who proceeded to storm off the set. The waiting around had obviously gotten to her.

"You're the fluffer," I said, looking at Susie. "You go get her."

Eventually Marlayna agreed to do the scene, but only as a voice-over; she refused to be on camera. With Pepper and Nina on the bed each holding a prop phone, Marlayna stood in a small adjacent bathroom with a microphone and delivered her lines. I was just beginning to lose myself in her bossy cocksucking story when Debi tossed me some lingerie and said, "We need a stand-in for the cutaway shots of Marlayna in her office. Get dressed." And then, I heard my mother say, "Please, Lisa, whatever you do out there in California, don't *star* in one of those porno movies!" I gave Debi my look of righteous criticism.

"Nobody's even gonna see your face."

I put on black lace stockings, thigh-high black leather boots, and a black sport bra and walked into the "office," which was just another room in the house where we'd hung up a nearly life-size poster of Vanessa Williams, the recently dethroned Miss America, in bondage. I sat in a chair with my back to the camera. "Put your feet up on the desk," Debi directed. "Now grab the phone and move around a little bit, like you're talking."

I bobbed my head and wiggled around in my seat. No? No. Too teenybopper. More aggressive? Okay. I conjured up Marlayna's bitchy commands in my head, winding and re-winding the parts where, in her Long Island accent, she said, "Take some *maw* you little *hoo-er!*" and "Wrap *yaw* lips around the head of my *cawk!*" Inspired, I picked up a black rubber dildo that was lying on the desk and whapped it against my thigh. Whap! Whap! Whapwhapwhapwhapwhapwhap!

"CUT!" yelled Debi. "I think we got it."

Around seven o'clock, we started getting ready for the big three-way with Sharon Mitchell as the leather butch escort. The thing I liked about Mitch was that even though she'd been in hundreds of films, she didn't look like a porn star. She was tall and thin, no curves. She had short dark hair, a big nose, an angular jaw and a generous mouth. Even in makeup she was handsome, not pretty. Her career was built on making straight porn movies, but whether she was, in her personal life, straight or gay or something in between, I wasn't sure.

Gay, straight and bisexual were increasingly inadequate labels for the people I knew: lapdancers who made a living grinding on men's crotches but identified themselves as lesbians; porn stars who considered themselves straight even though they slept with both men and women on camera; gay and lesbian editors who worked at straight sex magazines like *Adam* and *Playboy,* respectively. Even Debi, who had been in a long-term lesbian relationship with Fatale producer Nan Kinney, was now planning her wedding to a biological man. Susie, America's Most Famous Lesbian Sexpert, was pregnant — and it happened the old-fashioned way. And what about me? I was working at a lesbian sex magazine, but I wasn't a lesbian. How could I — or anyone — separate sex life from sex work?

For some the answer is "It's a living." Others would say, "Because everyone in this business is bisexual whether they know it or not. That's how!" The thinking being that any straight or gay person who's had even one crossover experience or even *thought* about it is technically bisexual and that's what allows them to breeze back and forth over the fence of sexual convention. While it's true that many of us "in the business" have had bisexual experiences for love or money or both, I believe the larger explanation is this: People who are interested in sex and who choose to pursue their interest professionally tend to appreciate sexual expression in all of its forms. Sexuality itself is what's fascinating and sexual preference is, in many cases, less relevant.

Whatever her label, this scene called for Mitch to strap on a big lavender dildo and start by taking Nina from behind while Nina went down on Pepper. But first, a few public service announcements about safe sex. "Our body fluids will keep a safe distance from each other," Mitch said, trying to sound as commanding as possible. The intention was admirable — necessary, even — but the line flopped because it's nearly impossible to integrate that kind of overt political correctness into an erotic scene. Then Nina put a 4×4 battleship-gray latex square between Pepper's legs and started licking. It looked completely unsexy. *Maybe if the latex was pink . . . or clear . . .*

"Cut!" someone shouted. "Phone's ringing."

It was the garage lesbians, as we liked to call them, the two butches who were supposed to have sex on a weight bench in the garage while Nina peeped through a keyhole. Later the scene would be cut in as a flashback. But now they were calling to cancel at the last minute. Debi held the phone away from her head so we could all hear Garage Lesbian 1 give us her hysterical sob story about how she and her girlfriend — Garage Lesbian 2 — just broke up minutes ago and now she's going home to live with her mother and doesn't anybody care! (I have since discovered that no-shows and flakes are the rule rather than the exception.) Then Debi looked me straight in the eye and said, "It's you and me in the garage."

Dear Penthouse: *I once heard that porn stars are often required to fuck people they're not sexually attracted to and don't like very much. Needless to say, I never thought it would happen to me.*

I tried to talk, but only little gasping breaths came out. My thoughts, which were not making their way out of my mouth, were *No Fucking Way.* I'm not going to have sex with you in a garage — or anywhere. Even if you looked like Catherine Deneuve, I still wouldn't do it because I don't want to do it. I'm too self-conscious. I'm not an exhibitionist! Besides, neither one of us is a bulldyke.

So we stayed like that, with me emotionally suspended by the power of her psychic grip, until the sound of the neighbor's dog yapping reached an insane crescendo and Debi looked away. I slumped against the wall, relieved. Suddenly, Debi ran to the window, stuck her head out and started screaming,

"SHUT UP!" at the top of her lungs. Mary, the camera operator, sensing my terror, pulled Debi away from the window and said, "It's okay, Debi. We'll reschedule the garage scene for some other time, no problem. "

We resumed filming. During the interruption, the stars had relaxed but stayed in position. Now Mitch dipped her fingers in a glass of water to refresh the lube on her dildo. Pepper made a joke in low tones and Nina cracked up. "QUIET ON THE SET!" Then, in a soft helpful voice, Debi proceeded to give the talent some direction.

"One time I was on the set of a million-dollar porn movie and the director walked off right at this point," Susie whispered in my ear. "She was a former children's theater director and when it came time for the sex, she just couldn't take a blow job scene putting a damper on her Shakespearean porn epic."

"ACTION!"

The room collapsed into silence, held up only by the sounds of heavy breathing punctuated with the occasional "oh yeah . . . that's it" or the click-and-wind of a still camera. On the monitor, I watched the video camera pan from the performers' bodies to their reflections on a wall of mirror squares splattered with gold flecks. Their faces pulled up into cloudless expressions of pleasure. *Amazing how they can turn it on and off for the camera so easily. Is it real? Does it matter as long as it looks real?* At that point, I could not care less. I was hungry, pissed off and sick of schlepping extension cords. The only thing hot was the lights. Funny how the *idea* of making a porn film and the reality are so far apart.

But as I sat there watching Mitch's cock going in and out

of Pepper's cunt while Nina sat on Pepper's face, my mind preoccupied with a million mundane details, my body began picking up tiny blips of arousal. I was getting aroused in spite of myself, and the wet rush between my legs took me somewhere beyond inhibitions and cameras and sexual politics. For a brief moment, I was alone with the essence of sex, in all of its unguarded glory. In a way, it was like having an orgasm. I was conscious of my surroundings and then, suddenly, the walls fell down and everything disappeared and I was floating in some nameless, ecstatic place. And, just like a good orgasm, it abruptly came to an end. The sexiness of it all faded away until it was nothing left but three naked bodies slapping against each other in a room.

And someone shouted, "It's a wrap!"

• • •

The life lessons at *On Our Backs* were priceless but they didn't pay the rent. So in between editorial shifts at the magazine, I waited tables and hit up every editor in town for work. Through a friend of a friend, I got a gig writing for a sex newsletter fashioned after *Penthouse Forum,* only with more of an educational bent. My pieces started out with some proper information on the subject at hand — genital piercing, masturbation, anal sex — but quickly degenerated into the filthiest scenarios I could think of. I didn't waste time coming up with stupid euphemisms like *ball gravy* or *tight oral passage,* but made sure that each piece contained some key ingredients: the women always had big orgasms, and they called the shots even when they were tied to the bed. I wrote each piece under a different pseudonym, but the endings were signature. Somebody took a hot load in the face and the narrator summed it all up with a gee-whiz one-liner dotted with an exclamation mark! The stories paid two hundred bucks a pop and I wrote about fifty of them. The faster I wrote, the more lucrative it was, and soon I had my time down to one intriguing hour per story.

My first real journalistic assignment was, conveniently, an interview with Susie for a local arts and entertainment magazine called *Frisko*. Tape recorder and notepad in hand, I asked such original questions as "Are you a feminist?" "How did *On Our Backs* get started?" and "Do you consider yourself dangerous?" But for the first time I asked Susie the question that so many have since asked me: Why do you write about sex?

"I have a great belief in sex having a certain truth and honesty to it that often upsets conventional political equations. Yet traditional feminism and the New Left politics that I grew up with were always very frightened to talk about sex explicitly. So I found my niche," she said.

Until I met Susie, I was never able to spell out why I was so attracted to the idea of sex as a public subject. I knew that speaking out about my own sexual experiences was cathartic. Discussing sex in public — especially the most private details — was a way to dole out sexual information and to chip away at the massive stone of guilt and shame. Of course sex talk was also fun, solipsistic, socially deviant, spiritually revelatory and it could even do what so many magazine headlines promised: Improve Your Sex Life.

But while it's great to swing from the chandelier, wear leather and find your G-spot, narcissism is not the bottom line.

In my book, sexual freedom is right up there with life, liberty and the pursuit of happiness.

• • •

One afternoon Susie called an editorial meeting to announce her departure from the magazine. She had recently published her first book, *Susie Sexpert's Lesbian Sex World,* given birth to a beautiful baby girl, Aretha, and was moving on to the next chapter of her life. Debi — who'd just returned from her honeymoon — couldn't believe the news. But disbelief turned to jealousy and eventually into a lawsuit. Debi charged Susie with corporate conflict of interest along with a laundry list of other violations. It was a knock-down, drag-out legal battle that would last two years, destroy their friendship and finally end in a draw.

Shortly after Susie resigned, I quit. Not only was I exhausted by the recent office politics, but I'd been working at *On Our Backs* for nearly two years and I was tired of writing only about lesbian sex. I wanted to talk about all kinds of sex, I wanted to . . . well, I didn't know exactly. Be a sex columnist? Therapist? Write box cover copy for porn videos? (Hey, somebody does it.) Or maybe I should just do something sensible, like go work for the post office. My mother deluged my answering machine with career advice. "Lisa? [long pause] It's me. Why don't you become a TV anchorwoman? I just love that Diane Sawyer. She has such nice hair. . . ."

4

The Future of Sex

THE FUTURE OF SEX appeared to me in the fall of 1991 in the shape of one desk, one phone, no staff and a pile of articles left behind by my predecessors, who wandered off leaving things half-finished. My first day as editor of *Future Sex* magazine, I thumbed through the manuscripts. One was a piece about having sex using a new technology called Virtual Reality, some kind of rubber suit and helmet combo that hooked up to a computer and would simulate in 3-D any sexual experience you could dream up, kind of like an erotic, IBM-induced acid trip. There were several pieces of fiction, one about a woman being sexually serviced by a robot and another about — well, I still don't know what it was about — people who got Sennheiser microphones shoved under their skin before they jerked off. There were a few other futuristic predictions and lots of nude color pictures of "Natalie," an Asian woman with very large, all-natural breasts posing with various accoutrements: swim goggles, a fish net, a length of rope.

The publishers of the magazine were two fortysomething guys: Bill Weiss, a Jewish personal injury lawyer, and Martin Leung, a Chinese doctor, looking for something fun to do with their spare change. I was the third editor they'd hired after sci-fi author/screenwriter John Shirley took the money and ran and R. U. Sirius left to edit *Mondo 2000*. Initially I was contacted by Shirley to write an article for *Future Sex*, but when the magazine never materialized and I never got paid, I started dialing for dollars. The next thing I knew, I was being offered the job.

The original business proposal described *Future Sex* as a sex magazine for·men, complete with service articles about high-tech gear, science fiction, a sports car review section titled "Auto-Erotica" and an exclusive pictorial focus on naked Asian women. I thought the concept was pretty stupid, but any port in a storm — I'd been unemployed for months. More important, the magazine was directionless; it was being cobbled together piece by attenuated piece. I believed I could step in and steer it toward a more original destination.

I worked in the Grant Building, an architectural landmark that had survived the 1906 earthquake, and it had a distinct gumshoe feel to it. The hallways were marble, and venetian blinds hung over the windows at uneven angles. There was a transom over every door, and each occupant's name was stenciled in black lettering on the pebbled glass. It stood at the corner of 7th and Market in the heart of San Francisco's dismal Tenderloin district. I called it the Corner of Insanity because it seemed to attract every unmedicated mental patient in a mile radius. Next door to the Grant Building was my namesake,

Lisa House, a dirt-cheap, bowel-blasting Chinese take-out joint followed by Merrill's drugstore, where a loitering lunatic once tried to stab exiting patrons in the eye with a fork. Capping our end of the long block was the Market Street Cinema, a strip club specializing in women with FFF breasts.

I often started my day by wading through the throng of hustlers, dealers and people screaming to themselves to grab a cup of coffee before I stepped around a puddle of vomit on my way through the front door and took the maddeningly slow elevator to the seventh floor where, on warm days, the aroma of sun-baked urine from Piss Alley wafted all the way up. My desk was in one rented corner of the office of the political satire magazine *The Nose*. Edited by the cigar-smoking Jack Boulware, *The Nose* ran stories like "It's Beginning to Look a Lot Like an Exit Wound: The First-Ever Comprehensive Guide to JFK Conspiracy Christmas Gifts" and "Fathers Know Best — Albuquerque's Infamous Halfway House for Pedophile Priests."

When I first signed on as *Future Sex* editor, I didn't know much about future technology and, frankly, I didn't care. I wasn't *into* computers. I never read Robert Heinlein. I didn't even watch *Star Trek*. I just wanted a chance to create a forward-thinking sex magazine. What the hell was "high-tech sex" anyway? Computer porn? Fucking robots? Maybe we'll all live on Tang, grow babies in test tubes and rub Orbs to have orgasms. Like, wow, man. Ever notice how the Digital Age looks a lot like the Space Age?

Part of my disdain was, admittedly, rooted in fear. I've been afraid of technology ever since I was a sophomore in high school and my biology partner, Michelle, stuck a pair of metal tweezers into the electric socket mounted on top of our workstation. Our teacher was droning on about the reproductive systems of worms and I was writing some boy's name over and over in my notebook and Michelle was just idly twirling the tweezers around, making little carvings in the black rubber desktop, and then — ZAP! There were screams and blue sparks and smoke, and I thought, *This shit could kill you!* (Although all we got were detentions.) So how could technology, which I always viewed as alienating, densely mathematical and potentially deadly, possibly enhance the highly sensual experience of sex?

One Friday night after work I was in the Berkeley hills at a *Mondo 2000* party, the fringe art + technoculture journal that launched a thousand cyberpunks, doing smart drugs (remember those?) and talking to a guy named Ron Gompertz. (A transplanted New York Jew, Ron looks not unlike David Duchovny from *The X-Files,* but with less hair.) He told me he ran the indie rock label Heyday Records, and also dabbled in this high-tech recording technology he called Virtual Audio, or 3-D sound. Then he popped The Question.

"So, what do you do?"

"I'm a pornographer."

He choked on his glass of Fast Blast. "We should make a triple-X 3-D CD," he joked weakly, after composing himself.

Handing him my number I told him I'd be very interested in hearing an audio demonstration and, possibly, more than that. Ron walked me to my truck and stood in the driveway as I pulled away. "She's cute," he told a friend after I left. "Too bad for me she's a lesbian."

A week later I arrived at Ron's house in the middle of the afternoon for the demo and, lo and behold, had the same gay thoughts about him. He was thirty-eight, lived alone with his dog and owned a beautiful home in Noe Valley (one neighborhood up from the Castro) that was so tastefully decorated I felt like I was walking into the Pottery Barn catalog.

Ron answered the door wearing a faultless all-Gap ensemble and warmly shook my hand. I plopped down in a comfortable armchair and we made small talk while he cued up the DAT tape. He handed me a blindfold, the kind they give you on airplanes, and a pair of headphones and instructed me to put them both on, which I did.

"Whenever you're ready, I'll start the tape," he said.

"Ready," I nodded and waited for the show to begin. But first, the doorbell rang, inciting Morgan, Ron's high-strung English cocker spaniel, to attack the front door. I could hear his crazed *ggrrrr-YAP! ggrrrr-YAP!* as he skidded across the room, his toenails powerless against the hardwood floor. *Why isn't Ron answering the door?* After a minute or so Morgan accepted defeat and trotted off to another room. Then I heard the clicking of Ron's boots as he approached and circled around me. He stopped, silent. I felt him breathe in my ear. Standing behind me, he picked up a box of wooden matches and shook them around my head, the subtlest of threats. Lighting one, he let it sizzle so close to me I could smell it burning. I was trying to decide whether I enjoyed this little game or not, when I heard scissors cut up the air just inches from my head. *Holy shit, he's another John Wayne Gacy!* I tore off the blindfold, ready to deck my host, but I found I was completely alone.

"Ron?" I called out.

"Yeah?" He was carrying an Alessi tray of coffee and biscotti from the kitchen into the living room.

I sunk down into the chair, agog.

"Pretty neat, huh?" he said, reading my face.

As I snacked, Ron unveiled the recording device itself and explained the technology.

"Virtual Audio is based on a computer-enhanced binaural recording system that samples sound in 360 degrees," Ron said, caressing the gear like Carol Merrill. "Using dummy head synthesis technology, it picks up sound the way the human ear does." The recording equipment looked like a life-size head and shoulders on a tripod. It was faceless, covered in a soft gray material, and there were two small rubber ears that housed the actual microphones. "Unlike stereo, where sound comes from either the left or the right, Virtual Audio provides spatial cues telling you if the sound is in front of you, behind you, close or far away. And it's digital — there's no analog tape hiss — so when you're listening, it feels like *you are there.*"

"But how come I *felt* you breathing in my ear and I *smelled* that match?"

"That's called the 'psychoacoustic effect,' which happens when one sense is tricked into believing the cue is real and the other senses follow along in pursuit. Because the match sounded so real, it smelled real, too."

Ron went on to describe Virtual Reality, using the words *multisensory* and *fully immersive* and *Jaron Lanier.* Like Virtual Audio, VR is also a computer-generated simulation of a three-dimensional environment but focuses on being fully immersive, meaning that all of your five senses, particularly sight and touch, are tricked into believing what they're experiencing is real. By wearing special goggles and a glove — the most famous of which were the EyePhones and Datagloves developed by computer scientist Jaron Lanier — a person could submerge herself in an artificial world and interact with it. The type of interactive experience depended on the application: a military flight simulation, a medical procedure, an architectural walk-through, a shoot-'em-up video game.

"What about the erotic applications?" I asked.

Ron coughed. And looked at the floor. And blushed. "They, uh, don't exist. Yet."

In the next twenty-four hours, not only would I discover that Ron was absolutely heterosexual when — during a mutual listen to a bizarre demo tape by *Mondo* entouragist Lady Sarah Drew titled "The Vulvic Ring Cycle" — we started making out, but I would also become his business partner. We named our new company Algorithm and soon began laying down tracks for *Cyborgasm,* an anthology of erotic scenes and music recorded in Virtual Audio.

As producer, my vision for *Cyborgasm* was this: no scripts. I wanted spontaneity. I wanted people to improvise erotic fantasies or true experiences; I wanted to record them masturbating or having sex with another person. And just exactly how would I find these people? By flipping through my Rolodex. My first phone call was, of course, to Susie Bright.

The inaugural session took place at Ron's house. Out back, there was a redwood deck and hot tub along with a very small separate room that we decided to use as a recording space. In the spirit of the times, I asked Susie if she wouldn't mind performing on a dose of GHB. Known on the emerging cyber scene as a "smart aphrodisiac," GHB (gamma-hydroxy buty-rate) modified the amount of dopamine released in the brain, producing a variety of subtle effects including mild relaxation, an increased desire to talk and dance, greater sexual sensitivity. Perfect! Susie, an LSD aficionado from way back, agreed — out of skepticism. "Smart drugs,"she scoffed. "Like they're really gonna do anything."

I mixed what looked like a few white chips of plastic in a glass of water until they dissolved.

"Are you sure that's enough?" Susie asked.

"The guy, the dealer, said to start out with just a little bit. Here." Susie downed the glass and let out a little burp. "How's it taste?"

"Gross."

We all went back to the recording room and Ron set up the Head in the middle of the floor. He did a level check and then disappeared behind a floor-to-ceiling partition to man the DAT deck and monitor Susie's performance through headphones.

Susie and I sat around the Head, waiting for the drugs to kick in.

"Feel anything?"

"Nothing."

"Okay, well let's just start then."

She began to tell a story about kneeling down in a confessional booth and telling a priest all about her sins. Five minutes into it, she began having trouble getting her words out.

". . . and the priest's . . . [HUGE breath] hands . . . were on his . . . [swallow, GASP] cock. . . ." I noticed her eyes were losing their focus. "Do you need some water?" I asked, at which point she fell forward, grabbing my hair and sticking her tongue in my mouth on the way down.

"I'm havin' the biggest rush right now," she whispered as she felt me up.

I responded enthusiastically, thinking, IT'S REAL SEX IN VIRTUAL AUDIO! Anything for a good take. Sixty seconds later, she pulled away. Her face was green and she said, "I think I'm gonna puke." She could barely manage to crawl toward the sliding glass door and stick her head out for air. Meanwhile the tape is still rolling and Ron has not come out from behind the magic curtain.

"Ron! Cut! Call the smart drug dealer and get the antidote!" I shouted as I knelt beside Susie and held her hair back. Finally Ron appeared with this look — was it shock? — on his face. He hovered above us, not saying anything.

"Ron? Go call!" He walked into the house.

"Is Ron mad at me?" Susie asked softly.

"Mad? Of course not. I'm sure he's just very concerned."

We spent the rest of the afternoon taking care of Susie and listening to our dealer's explanation of how GHB was extremely dose-sensitive and that finding the right amount was often a difficult and individual matter. As soon as Susie felt well enough to go home, Ron and I couldn't wait to find our right amounts. We took one quarter of Susie's dose. Nothing. Then half, then double, then triple. Then it was all gone and we sat on the couch with nothing but stomachaches. Then Ron got that look on his face again.

"What? Are you mad that the drugs aren't working for us?"

"No."

"Are you mad that we didn't get any work done today?"

"No."

"Are you mad that Susie got sick?"

"Getting warmer."

"That she kissed me?"

"*I* almost felt like puking when I heard that going on. How could you!" He took off flying around the living room. I wasn't sure if he was upset by the fact that I made out with a *girl* or just that I made out with another *person,* so I badgered him with lots of little questions. Was it this? Was it that?

"It's all of the above!" he shouted, waving his arms to indicate the monstrous dimensions of his disgust.

"But Ron, two women together is the number one male fantasy in America!"

"Well, I'm not every man."

"I'll say."

He circled around and around and finally landed back on the couch again. And we sat there, arms crossed, eyes forward, for a long time. How we continued working on this X-rated project remains somewhat of a mystery to me. Even more mysterious is the fact that one year later, Ron would ask me to marry him and I would say yes.

• • •

Things at *Future Sex* got off to an equally rocky start. My first item of business was to come up with two additional pictorials to complete the first issue. The publishers specifically wanted layouts that featured Asian women — no men — and it was my job to find them. This raised a cluster of sensitive issues for me. First, I was all for sexual diversity and was sincerely interested in presenting bold images of Asian women, but I didn't know how to go about it. I wasn't part of the Asian community, I didn't have the social connections, I didn't personally know any Asian women I could approach for this kind of thing. The fact is, bringing racial diversity to pornography is much more difficult than it sounds — and feminist pornography is no exception.

When I was at *On Our Backs,* readers were always clamoring for more color. Why don't you show more Latinas? More Asians, blacks, Native Americans? And the truth was, we would if we could. But finding women of color who were interested in contributing was difficult. Like the feminist movement itself, feminist pornography has largely been a middle-class, white women's scene, and encouraging nonwhite women to participate in it has always been a struggle. When a white editor decides to promote erotic multiculturalism it's tricky because it involves not only discussing but *eroticizing* race and class, two extremely touchy subjects.

Second, I didn't want to be involved with perpetrating offensive stereotypes about female Asian sexuality. While race can certainly be an erotic charge, there was no way I was going to cultivate images of Me-So-Horny or Oriental Dolls. Besides, there is nothing inherently futuristic about Asian women, and the idea of displaying them as some kind of twenty-first-century exotica really creeped me out.

And third, the No Men rule was ridiculously passé. How could a magazine claim to represent the future of sex and then not even show a little hot couples' action?

Finally after several weeks of searching, a friend of the publishers introduced me to a potential candidate. Angelina was a vibrant young hardbody with olive skin and bee-stung lips, who appeared to be a stunning mix of Vietnamese and African-American. When I quizzed her on her motivation, expectations, creative ideas and sexual limits, she was raring to go. "Maybe we could shoot the pictures in a butcher shop and I could lie nude on a side of beef!" she suggested. Immediately I dialed Phyllis Christopher, one of the best erotic photographers I've ever worked with, and asked her to do the shoot. I wanted something edgy, apocalyptic. We location-scouted for several days along the San Francisco Bay's decomposing shipyards looking for a spot that was accessible yet private. I hired a hair stylist and a makeup artist and begged several boutiques to loan us clothes for the shoot.

After all this work lay the final hurdle: the publishers' approval process. Because it was, after all, their money, the publishers had to approve the talent whenever I assigned a shoot. Basically the process consisted of the publishers meeting the models and personally deciding if they were attractive enough to be in the magazine. (In the future, many, many models would get the buzzer at this point.) Both the meetings and the shoots had to be scheduled at the big spenders' convenience so they could attend and, on occasion, even play photographer. It was a major pain in the ass that dragged the entire creative process to an excruciating, grinding halt. This model, however, got the green light and the shoot was a go.

On Sunday morning, October 20, 1991, the photographer, the model, the stylists, the two publishers and I arrived at our remote industrial spot. Except we weren't the only ones. A large crowd was gathered at the water's edge looking across the bay, some through binoculars. *What are they doing? Bird-watching?* As it turns out, they were watching huge sections of Oakland and Berkeley burn to the ground. That would explain why it was raining ashes. Hot, dry east winds were speeding down from the crest of the Oakland–Berkeley hills at sixty-five miles per hour and swirling through five years of drought-dry brush and eucalyptus trees while temperatures soared into the nineties. It would become the nation's worst urban fire since the Great Chicago Fire of 1873.

But never mind this freaky commingling of sex and death — the show must go on! Under a toxic brown sky, Phyllis began shooting Angelina in leather fetish wear and a silver wig as she reclined provocatively over rusted rebar and graffitied rocks. Then I heard these distant click-click noises and turned to see that Bill Weiss, the balding ponytailed lawyer, had pulled out his pro camera gear and was taking his own pictures. I told him it was really uncool to cut in on Phyllis's action and, reluctantly, he put his camera away. Even more annoying, however, was Angelina's subsequent refusal to take her clothes off. Topless, yes. Bottomless, no. "That's not our agreement," I reminded her. She confessed that she felt uncomfortable with "so many people" standing around, and if they disappeared for a while she would undress.

Now it was late in the afternoon. Ash blanketed the top of my head like snow. The firegazers had gone home to watch the blaze on TV. The stylists split. The only ones left standing were the publishers. I walked over to them, explained the situation and politely asked if they wouldn't mind getting a cup of coffee so that soon we could all go home. The suggestion made Martin Leung, the doctor, absolutely furious. He was writing the checks! How dare this bitch tell him to get lost! Eventually, though, Martin slammed the door to his black-cherry Cadillac and sped off in a cloud of dust, leaving Bill to get lost all by himself until the shoot was finished.

In the end, the pictures weren't bad — for a fashion shoot. Despite our meticulous planning, the sexual energy mysteriously failed to be captured on film. Having a model who — scout's honor — assured me she was a total exhibitionist and then became positively inhibited at the eleventh hour certainly didn't help. While the photographs were quite artful, they lacked both the explicitness and sense of genuineness that, to me, are essential characteristics of good pornography. Still, I considered the shoot a keeper and was ready to move on to pictorial number 3, so I was rather surprised when the publishers told me they were killing it. Not for editorial reasons, but because of their newfound personal dislike of Angelina.

In June 1992, the magazine went to press. The cover of the premiere, glossy issue featured "Natalie" with her naked back to the camera, holding a butcher knife along with this copy: "Cutting-Edge Erotica, Electronic Masturbation, Cyborg Love Slaves and 3-D Digital Orgasms" and a yellow snipe that read "Asian Beauty" — a slight improvement from the original "Asian Beauties."

The photo spreads included "Natalie," and "Portfolio," a showcase of single images from a variety of photographers, including Charles Gatewood, Annie Sprinkle and Phyllis Christopher — one shot of Angelina making muscles against a backdrop of smoke. Substituting for the Angelina pictorial was "Salonge," a barely-legal-looking woman lounging around in lacy white lingerie with pink bows. They were sent to me by a photographer with the pseudonym Joe King. Over the phone he told me, "It's like *joking,* get it? It's a joke." I had the "Salonge" photos digitally manipulated, fuzzing out the background and leaving the model in sharp focus. At the time, I thought the bells and whistles of Photoshop would be a loud enough distraction from the cliché content.

The first issue also contained all of those articles I came across on my first day plus a few new ones: an essay on the latest cinematic styles in pornography, several erotic book reviews and my editorial. In it I wrote, "The most popular demand for tomorrow's sex world is this: intelligence. And not the artificial kind."

Brains, however, ain't much of a story. The story was wacky, madcap computerized perversity! The moment *Future Sex* hit the newsstands, the phone started ringing and it never stopped.

The tabloid TV show *Hard Copy* was first in line. Sandwiched in between a piece about a man who kidnapped a busload of schoolchildren and a transsexual involved in a murder plot was a story about the magazine. "Imagine sex in the future," said the announcer. "Imagine erotic magazines without a Hef or a Gooch or a Larry Flynt at the helm. Imagine this woman, a baby-faced yuppie . . ." *Yuppie?* Over a zippy montage of words lifted from the magazine like "eroto-tronics" and "cyborgas" (obviously missing the "m") I talked about trying to create progressive pornography, but the situation was futile. After all, I had just signed my name to a magazine filled exclusively with nude women and science projects that didn't exist. But the biggest media bomb was dropped by the *New York Times*. The headline read: "Space-age gadgets + sexual fantasies = cybersex" and the article crowned me the "queen of high-tech porn." My fate, it seemed, was sealed.

Closer to home, less diplomatic reviews were pouring in. I bumped into author Kathy Acker on the street one day and whipped out a copy of *Future Sex* from my bag. She took one look at "Salonge," laughed out loud in disbelief and asked, "What's with the mail-order bridal finery?" Jude Milhon, an editor at *Mondo 2000* who contributed the fictional piece about robot-sex, tore into me over the telephone about how unenlightened the magazine was and how she wished she had never been part of it. *San Francisco Weekly* columnist Laura Fraser wrote, "There's no political consciousness behind this — as there is behind *On Our Backs* — just a marketing strategy," and like so many of my friends she wondered, "What happened? Maybe the male publishers gave Palac her own exciting, intelligent column and photo-op upfront and then bound and gagged her while they put out the rest of the magazine." *Honey, if you only knew.* Yet her criticism was also proactive. Sick and tired of images of physical perfection, she offered to pose for *Future Sex,* "just to see a body like mine." The publishers' response: What does she look like? Is she fat? If she's fat, forget it.

Although Camille Paglia did write me a fan letter praising the magazine — "My favorite sequence was 'Salonge' — very hot!!!" — it wasn't enough to change what I knew to be true: In its current incarnation, the magazine sucked. In the interest of public relations, I kept my mouth shut about what was going on behind the scenes but I was running out of justifications like "It was the first issue and first issues are never perfect." I was filled with insatiable optimism and total despair. I didn't come all this way to hear a couple of good ol' boys with fat wallets tell me a woman is TOO FAT or TOO UGLY to be sexually appealing, and to hand me a list of adolescent sexual fantasies that I was supposed to help fulfill in order to ease their midlife crises. I was hired to be the editor, not the toady.

On the other hand, I didn't want to lose my woefully underpaid job. I believed in the importance of creating a magazine where sexual desire and sexual identity could be discussed and depicted. And I was determined to do something better with the next issue.

• • •

The first step toward something better was assembling a staff. Our nascent, part-time editorial team consisted of Curium Design, run by brother/sister Bennington grads Evan and Joy Sornstein, who engineered the magazine's techno-organic, Neville Brody–inspired art direction; my good friend and journalist Laura Miller as senior editor, who kept her day job as publicist for Good Vibrations; and Allison Diamond, full-time office manager of *The Nose,* as multimedia editor.

The second was to bring in the advertising dollars to pay the staff, since the first issue had only six ads, two of which were complimentary. Because of the magazine's technosex angle, we gained a few unique clients like Paradise Electro Stimulations, a collection of sex toys that zapped your genitals with electrical current, or the Motorized Orgasmic Release machine, an automatic penis-sucker that retailed for $895. But Absolut Vodka? I wish. The more explicit the content, the more advertising dollars you lose. We relied on adult video, CD-ROM and phone sex companies to pay the bills and, unfortunately, many of their ads featured the most unimaginative orifice close-ups with the crudest, rudest copy splattered all over them.

The third step was to improve the photographic content. Sometimes I think a sex magazine could be filled with columns of blahblahblah and most people wouldn't notice or care. It's the pictures that make all the difference, and I told the publishers as much by waving all the reviews in their faces and insisting that if there was to be a future for us then we better start moving forward.

I organized a shoot that called for a man and a woman to slowly undress and get it on at dusk in Golden Gate Park while "Cameraboy," the photographer we'd hired, shot them paparazzi-style with a long lens and high-speed film. After much heated deliberation, I was allowed to include nudes of Laura Fraser in the bathtub reading *The Nation,* cuddling with her kitten and dancing with her beau. We bought an essay by ex-porn star Richard Pacheco titled "What, Me Impotent?"

about his faltering erections on the set and illustrated it with a photo of him nude inside a deli cooler filled with cheeses and kosher bologna. In the accompanying photo for my editorial, titled "Getting Behind the Future," I'm in underwear and combat boots grinding against a man's lusciously naked ass as he bends over for me. All in all there were — count 'em! — eleven naked men slated to run in the second issue.

Of course not every erotic shoot ended up being erotic. We took chances on fashion photographers who didn't know how to give sexual direction, which resulted in models standing in their underwear asking, "Um, what should I do?" Male models had trouble getting or maintaining an erection. Women chickened out at the last minute. There seemed to be no way to fully prepare for the emotional involutions that arise when people nude up for the camera, except just to do it. But even when things were flambé on the set, the pictures often came back looking inert, stale, the eroticism lost in the translation to the two dimensional.

The fourth and final step in my improvement program was my full-on investigation of this intersection between sex, technology and culture. San Francisco 1992 was the epicenter of all things cyber — space, punk, culture, sex — and I was, in every sense, wired. (Originally, *cyber* referred to the study of how computers process information but now described anything or anyone that seemed futuristic and cool.) The word on the street was that the Internet was on par with fire and the wheel, that the digital revolution was going to permanently transform the way we communicate because it would offer everyone unprecedented access to information. Since sex, at its core, is about communication, I was jazzed.

I started reading: Howard Rheingold, Timothy Leary, Terence McKenna, Brenda Laurel. I joined The WELL (Whole Earth 'Lectronic Link), an online community based in San Francisco. I attended Virtual Reality Special-Interest Group meetings and checked out digital technology conferences and sampled a variety of head-mounted displays. I went to a rave. And along the way I was introduced to some of the most creative, forward-thinking people working with computer technology — artists, programmers, writers, musicians, geeks and bon vivants who explained the Digital Revolution to me.

As the world moves from analog to digital, all types of media — photos, words, movies, sounds — can be digitized, or broken down mathematically into a specific series of ones and zeros, and transmitted anywhere in the world by anyone with computer access. It's fast, it makes the means of production and distribution accessible, and it gives everyone the potential to be The Media. Unlike the pyramid schemes of newspapers, television and radio, where one source disseminates information to many people, the Internet and digital technology allow *many* people to exchange ideas with *many* people, without a lot of high costs.

Exactly how digital technology was revolutionizing philosophy in the bedroom was, naturally, a frequently asked question. At which point all media eyes turned to me, since I was now wearing a sign that read "High-Tech Sex Chick." They wanted to know and they wanted to know right now:

Q: What is cybersex?
A: Etymologically, it's a cousin of cyberspace, the famous environment dreamed up by William Gibson in his 1984 book *Neuromancer,* where the characters literally plug their brains in to a computer-generated world.

Technically, I define cybersex as any erotic encounter involving digital technology like pornographic CD-ROMs, kinky E-mail, cruising on the Internet, Virtual Audio sex, phone sex — depending on the fiber optics — even dirty faxes. Vibrators, motorized penis pumps and inflatable dolls belong to the Industrial Revolution.

Q: Tell us more about this crazy new concept!

A: Actually, the connection between sex and technology is as old as the hills. Whenever new technologies come along, people find erotic uses for them. It's human nature to improve on pleasure. The printing press put sexually explicit pictures in the hands of the masses, the VCR allowed millions to watch X-rated movies in private, and now digital technology is making its mark.

Q: So what kinds of things can we see?

A: You can look at sex CD-ROMS, although I think they're lame. The "interactivity" is nothing more than multiple choice — skip the plot and go straight to the crotch shots. Basically, the naked babe has moved from print to video to the digital realm. Big deal.

Q: What about the Virtual Reality sex suits?

A: Oh, they don't exist. The most exciting technology that's available today are computer bulletin board systems, BBSes, which can be linked to the Internet, which is an international network of computer networks. This is what's changing people's lives — words. Simple, ASCII text. And it is this particular form of cybersex that's cutting across physical and geographic boundaries and redefining our approach to relationships, our ideas about gender, eroticism, the definition of "community standards" — even sex itself.

Of course, there's this snobbery that anyone who would have online sex is a loser who's too homely or hopeless to find a real partner. But the truth is, not everyone's ready for physical intimacy. Painful relationship breakups, physical handicaps, geographic isolation, shyness and the risk of HIV infection all keep people from diving straight into bed with someone new. But their sexual desire doesn't go away. Going online creates a very intense sense of intimacy almost instantly, literally within minutes. Relationships develop at high-speed in reverse: first you know their heart and soul, then you see their body. This is completely unparalleled in the human saga of love.

Q: But what about the VR sex suits?

A: When people say they're having sex online, I mean, what are they really doing? They're having sex! Of course, what does it mean to "have sex"? There's the historical measuring stick — heterosexual intercourse — but what about a good spanking? Or dressing up in latex? Or masturbation? For a lot of people the psychological edge is much more exciting than actual penetration. Online sex is like Masturbation Plus because it is you and your own hand — or whatever you use — *and* erotic communication with another sentient being at the same time, even though the other person might be in Abu Dhabi or wherever.

Q: Right. But what about the sex suits?

A: I think Howard Rheingold is responsible for them. He wrote the book *Virtual Reality* — an excellent book on the development of VR technology — and in it he had a chapter where he dreamed up the idea of "teledildonics." I have to tell you, I've tried on a lot of goggles and gloves and I never experienced a blur between reality and simulated reality. Even the most sophisticated VR applications made me feel submerged in a cartoon world, rather than in a lifelike parallel universe.

Q: When do you think we'll get the suits?

A: I don't know. I don't care! Most women don't care about cybersex suits. They're still wondering if it's okay to use a vibrator or to look at pornography and figuring out how to have an orgasm. Men, on the other hand, are thinking, "Gee, what new thing can I do with my dick? I know! A sex suit!"

Besides, VR research and development is expensive and most of the funding for high technology comes from big corporations or the government, two groups hardly interested in improving people's sex lives. And even if VR sex *did* exist, the computer power it would take to generate the basic building block of intimacy — the kiss — would be mind-boggling. VR sexware is vaporware, meaning it doesn't exist. There's no there there.

At this point, I could sense their disappointment. Without the suits, there wasn't much to look at. And this is the problem — or benefit, really — of cybersex. It's about the experience of communication, the depth of imagination. Trying to explain cybersex with a picture of someone sitting at her computer is like trying to understand a great book by having the camera zoom in on all the pages.

Still, the letdown continued. Certain reporters were disappointed because the *Future Sex* headquarters didn't look like the *Starship Enterprise.* It was just an office complete with spilled coffee, back issues piled everywhere, foam peanuts from UPS boxes all over the carpet. I didn't parade around in a silver butt thong and spaceboots, or eat little pills for lunch or have a harem of slave boys with long tongues crawling around under my desk. The photographs in the magazine didn't show people having sex in the fourth dimension or in some never-before-captured-on-film sex position. But the biggest disappointment was No Suits.

Was I missing something? Maybe somewhere, somebody in their basement was conducting secret suit experiments. So I phoned Mike Saenz, the creator of *Virtual Valerie* and *Mac-Playmat,* two of the world's first X-rated computer games. He said the closest he'd come to a "boner machine" turned out to be nothing more than a line of increasingly explicit beaver shots taped to a friend's wall. In the spirit of parody, Saenz suggested we create our own phony VR sex gear and publish it in *Future Sex.* Give the people what they want!

On a bar napkin I made a stick-figure drawing of the woman's suit, a bra shaped like robot hands and a G-string with a huge vibrator attachment and lots of wires, and sent it off to Saenz at his 3-D animation company, Reactor. Saenz created a four-page spread titled "The Love Machine." It featured human models, a man and a woman, making porno faces, naked except for the Darth Vaderesque helmets, gloves and strap-on orgasmatrons. The accompanying article gave a timeline of projected advances in cybersex technology up to the year 2200 — when surgical implants became affordable — and was loaded with geek talk like "tactile data playback" and "simskin components."

"What's 'tempest-shielded'?" I asked him.

"It means that in the event of a nuclear attack, these suits will be left standing!" He cackled like a mad scientist.

The ridiculous His 'n' Hers technolingerie (hers was pink) was scheduled to appear on the second cover of *Future Sex* with the headline "Strap In, Tweak Out, Turn On!"

Oh, the monster I helped create.

Also scheduled for the second issue of *Future Sex* was a lively introduction to erotic BBSes and their users titled "Getting It Online" by Gary Wolf. (Wonderful Gary! One of the only writers we knew with a modem.) Since sexually explicit graphics are the main feature of so many BBSes, we decided to save our readers the money and time of downloading and show them exactly what this new computer porn looked like. (Back then, each image took at least thirty minutes to arrive.) A photo titled "Corndild" featured an ear of yellow niblets stuffed in a special place; "Chocock" showed an interracial blow job in a motel setting; and "Enails" was a close-up of four middle-aged female hands with inches-long frosted fingernails gripping a cock as if they were going up the neck of a baseball bat. Not surprisingly, these images weren't much different from the pages of an amateur porn magazine. But we admired the free spirit of the pioneering cyber-exhibitionists — so erotically democratic! Young, old, black, white, fat, skinny, suburbanite and hippie. And so, without a second thought, we sent the magazine to press.

The next thing I knew, I was on the phone with our printer in Lenexa, Kansas. "About those pictures on page forty-three," he said. "It's against our company policy to print pictures that show penetration or bodily fluids." This was the first time I'd ever heard anything about the great unwritten rule of sex magazine publishing: no penetration, no bodily fluids. It certainly explained why the erotic photo layouts in *Penthouse* and other national magazines (known as men's sophisticates) always seemed so fake, showing people on the verge of sex, rather than actually having it. His tongue is *almost* on her clit. Her lips are *about* to wrap around his cock. The dildo is *not quite* in. Sucking dildos, however, is still a gray area. While it's not illegal to show any of these things, doing so can lead to some unfavorable consequences.

The printer insisted that he, personally, didn't have a problem with any of the images but other people might. What if one of their Christian clients walked through the plant on a press check, caught a glimpse of the bodily fluids and decided to take his business elsewhere? And even if they printed *Future Sex* during the middle of the night — as they were now planning to do — what if an employee complained about being exposed to the images? He didn't want to "force" anyone to work on our "controversial" magazine. This kind of buck-passing extends well beyond the confines of sex magazines. It's the reason why we never see a woman's bare breast on the cover of, say, *Vogue* magazine. Is it illegal to show? No. But a woman's nipple might offend printers, distributors, advertisers, retailers and subscribers, whose displeasure can be measured in cash. When it comes to sex, it's always somebody else's problem.

I could have threatened to take my business elsewhere, except there was nowhere else to go. Dimension Graphics was the only place in the entire country we'd found to print our magazine, although for an outrageous price. Once a printer finds out the content is sex, the bill automatically skyrockets. It's their little extortion morality scheme of "Oh gee, it's against our policy to print anything we find sexually offensive — unless we can make a killing doing it." It's the same reason that X-rated videos cost more to rent. Yet sometimes even money is not enough. The main reason printers and distributors are reluctant to traffic in sex magazines is the fear of legal prosecution. Nobody wants to go to jail for producing or distributing *potentially* obscene material, or be driven out of business by the high cost of legal defense, so they set up certain avoidance strategies for protection. Of course, there's no way to know *in advance* if something is obscene. There is no federal statute that says, "Pictures of interracial sex are against the law" or "Pictures of women with corncobs in their cunts are against the law." The only exception is child pornography, which is outlawed by the federal government. In 1973, the Supreme Court (*Miller* v. *California*) decided that material was obscene and not protected under the First Amendment if (1) the average person, applying contemporary community standards, would find that the material arouses a "prurient interest," meaning an abnormal or obsessive interest; (2) the material depicts or describes in a patently offensive way sexual conduct specifically prohibited by applicable state law; and (3) the work, taken as a whole, lacks serious literary, artistic, political or scientific value. In order for something to be judged obscene, it must be taken to court and fail this three-prong test.

To fix our little problem, the printer offered to cover up the offending details with black dots. Not dots, exactly, but geometric shapes — or hearts — that he thought would fit right in with the "artsy" design of our magazine. There was silence on my end. He asked if I would rather have diamonds.

"Look, the problem's not the shape of the dots," I said, "it's the DOTS!"

Black dots. Another pitiful example of our limited definition of sex: It isn't sex until the hole gets filled. Even more pathetic is the fact that a black dot cleanses a sexually explicit image in the eyes of the law. If you can't see the exact locus of penetration, it isn't penetration, which means it probably won't be found obscene in court. Never mind that you can clearly tell what's going on from the rest of the picture. Like a modern fig leaf, the black dot claims to protect us from being shocked and offended by sex, when what it really does is reinforce the idea that what's behind the dot is shocking and offensive.

Finally, the printer agreed to run the uncensored photos — just this once — if we promised to follow the rules next time. But our victory was short-lived. The following week our largest national distributor dumped us, refusing to carry the issue with "hard-core" photos in it.

I quickly realized that it takes more than a fistful of bright ideas to create "something better" in terms of pornography. If you don't have a printer or a distributor, you don't have a magazine. And all the creativity in the world goes unnoticed when your labor of love is rotting in a warehouse in Kansas. But you know what? Even if the threat of prosecution wasn't hanging over anyone's head, even if the publishers of *Future Sex* were the greatest guys in the world and I had unlimited resources to create "good" pornography, there was no guarantee I could do it. There would still be critics sniffing the finished product saying, "That's not erotic!" and they very well might be right. Pornography, once created to fit the select desires of wealthy patrons, is now produced for mass consumption. Yet our erotic tastes have remained exactly the same: very, very particular.

So what makes pornography good? High production values? Realistic people in realistic sexual situations having believable orgasms? Presenting sex as a part of an intimate relationship? It can be all of those things and more. And less. Pornography doesn't have to be profound to turn me on. It doesn't have to aspire to be art. I appreciate the hyperreality of porn; the amalgam of fantastic people, situations without consequences and the unrealistically real sex makes the genre what it is. If a piece of pornography has the power to arouse me, I find value in that. But just because it was good for me doesn't make it good pornography. Good pornography is the thing that gives me insight into the human condition *and* makes me come. And that is tremendously difficult to create.

• • •

Although few people could actually buy the second issue of *Future Sex,* because of the distribution debacle, it became our landmark issue. *Cyborgasm* was released at roughly the same time, and featured performances by Susie Bright (her second successful attempt, titled "Circus Whore"), Annie Sprinkle, Don Bajema and a host of others. As a result, the editorial office hosted a constant parade of camera crews and photographers and reporters from all over the world hoping to try on the VR sex suits depicted on our cover.

It became clear to me that the media focus on the technology was mostly just a ruse to talk about sex. The "cyber" part validated the sex discussion. Everyone could pretend to be interested in the amazing new technology, in the same way that people claimed to read *Playboy* for the articles. The technology angle also implied that since it took brains to operate computers, cyberporn was going to be better and classier than the old fare.

Over and over I repeated: Cybersex isn't a replacement for face-to-face sensuality but an addition to it. The vibrator did not replace men, and cybersex will not replace real sex. Cybersex is not about having sex with a computer, but the exchange of erotic ideas between people. I pointed out that alienation existed long before the computer, so there would always be a marginal percentage who preferred their imagination to the real thing. Furthermore, why worry about how VR sex is going to fuck up people's lives when *real* sex is already doing a tremendous job of it?

In my second editorial, "Getting Behind the Future," I wrote, "The last sexual frontier isn't some intergalactic tactile data fuck: it's your ass." It was a frank column about anal sex and, whether he used a penis or she used a strap-on, how to get through the guilt-ridden issues surrounding it and enjoy it safely. It didn't mention computers or the word *cyber.* It was the most popular column I ever wrote. But did the media ever come around asking me to comment on the future of buttfucking? No.

For all the hype, however, the merging of sex and digital technology does provide substantial benefits, like unprecedented worldwide access to sex information. The Internet offers extensive resource materials about AIDS, STDs, pregnancy, contraception, infertility, impotence. Whatever kind of sexual support you need, you can find it online: gay and lesbian community forums, prostitutes' rights organizations, bondage newsgroups, Christian sexuality discussions, celibacy debates.

Moreover, cybersex itself has led to an increased cultural acceptance of masturbation as bona fide sex, not a sex substitute. Cybersex sanctioned mutual masturbation as something healthy and fun that could be practiced by people who weren't even in the same room. Digital technology transformed the idea that masturbation is something you do when you're a lonely loser who can't get laid into something that's hip, safe and cyber.

Cybersex isn't about a new kind of sex act or gadget. Cybersex is a fundamental change in the way we define the erotic experience.

• • •

At the height of the cybersex craze, Ron Gompertz asked me to marry him. Neither of us could stand the words *husband, wife, marriage* or *wedding,* yet somehow Ron and I believed our mutual distrust for the institution would see us through. We both wanted companionship, intimacy, children, that illusory sense of permanence. We were kind and compassionate and loyal toward one another — except for all the times when we were manipulative, condescending and felt like killing each other. Oh, the histrionics of love. Why not take the plunge? I said yes.

The minute I put that ring on my finger, though, things started to get ugly. The very qualities Ron was initially intrigued by — my suspicion of monogamy, my libido, my erotic fantasies, my professional interest in sex — were now thorns in his side. "Why can't you just be normal?" was his most frequent request, which I often fulfilled by going absolutely nuts: vicious criticism of his prudishness and his workaholic behavior, smashing dishes and all-around high drama. His follow-up was always the cool dagger: "Lisa. You're acting just like your mother."

Still, I was ready to go ahead and marry this man. Marriage had never been one of my top priorities, but love and commitment were. To cherish and love someone unconditionally, and to be loved and respected in the same way, is what I've always longed for. Now I felt I had to choose: myself or the relationship. I was twenty-nine years old. I wanted a partner. I wanted to have a child. And I so much wanted to be in love. So — despite all of my principles — I chose the relationship. I was willing to sacrifice my sexual identity because deep down I believed that no man would ever really love me if I didn't. "Sex isn't everything" and "nothing's perfect" were the anesthetics I used to dull the pain.

Two months later, I did the thing I swore I would never do: I threw the ring back in anger. I'd had a change of heart about sacrifice. A sacrifice is not — as Catholic school taught me — the act of relinquishing something highly valued in order to please. Sacrifice is forfeiture for the sake of the greater good. Under this definition, how could our relationship, which was filled with denial and resentment, possibly achieve any sort of greatness?

Ron and I managed to salvage our business relationship and eventually a friendship, too. I continued editing *Future Sex* and publicly advocating sexual independence, all the while wondering how a girl like me could end up so single. So when it came right down to it, I was a perfect candidate for cybersex. I wasn't getting laid, I liked to masturbate and I could type.

My parents' wedding. June 17, 1945.

Baby Lisa, age eighteen months.

My father, pontificating and puffing at the office.

First Holy Communion, with my mother. She still complains about "the face" I'm making in this picture every time she looks at it.

Fat and four-eyed in fifth grade. Possibly the worst photo of my entire life.

An early art school photo of our house in Chicago. I took it with my first camera, a gift from my father.

Age seventeen. You know what that means.

Me and college boyfriend Greg Graeff documenting our relationship in a Woolworth's photo booth.

Susie Bright reading *Magnet School,* taken the night of the G-string incident.

"Strap In, Tweak Out, Turn On!" The second issue of *Future Sex* featuring those wacky cybersex suits.

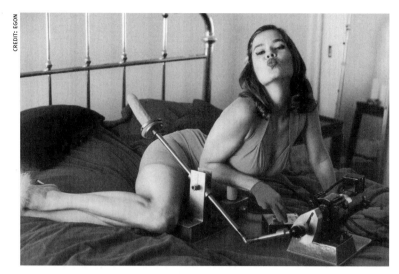

With, like, a sex machine.

Our *Cyborgasm* publicity shot.
That's Ron Gompertz wearing
the blindfold and headphones.

Susie Bright joins me in the sack during the "Do Me Feminist" shoot for *Esquire* magazine.

Andrew Rice and I tie the knot. April 25, 1997.

5

The Net Effect

WHEN I CRUISED IN cyberspace for the first time I, like so many red-blooded Americans, logged on from the office. I'd been offered complimentary accounts at several BBSes, so one night after work I set things up with Odyssey, an adults-only online service that featured thousands of X-rated GIFs, a matchmaking database, erotic forums, complete anonymity and lots of people looking to blow their wad.

I identified myself as F, female; listed my turn-ons as sushi and red lipstick; chose the naively honest online name Lisapal and started mingling in the group chat rooms marked Hot Adult, Anything Goes and Jacuzzi. Jacuzzi was, actually, very much like being welcomed into a hot tub of naked strangers who were all groping each other under the bubbles while they made provocative small talk. Literally between the lines of the group conversation, messages kept popping up that only I could read, inviting me to "go private." Like someone whispering in my ear, a string of text appeared: "Would you like to go someplace quiet, just the two of us, where we could ;) talk?" The frequency and the implication of these invitations — all from men — was overwhelming. I was scared to go private! What was I supposed to say? To do? What if someone said something mean to me? What if I got bored? Yes, I knew that if the situation got uncomfortable I could simply shut my computer off, but I couldn't delete the experience. I logged off.

I spent the next twenty-four hours working up my courage to try it again. You're being ridiculous, I told myself, go grab the world by the ass! So that evening I dialed in and after some heavy flirting with GI Joe, I boldly asked him to go private. He responded with hesitation — but only for a moment. Once we were alone, GI said he wanted us to "get to know" each other. I wanted to get off but saw no reason for the two to be mutually exclusive. I talked about how I enjoyed going to strip joints and throwing money down. He'd never heard of a woman who did that. I talked about the kinds of porn I liked to watch. He'd never heard of a woman who did that either. I assumed my unusual interests were wowing him, so I cut to the chase and told him to unzip his pants and grab his cock. In all caps he responded, WHAT ARE YOU, SOME KIND OF FAGGOT? And then he disappeared forever.

Why can't I just be normal?

A few nights later, I tried a different approach. I logged on to ECHO (East Coast Hang Out), a Manhattan-based arts and ideas salon run by Stacy Horn, using my real name. Almost immediately, a greeting appeared on my screen. I was being

Yo'ed by Hadley, Stephen Hadley.* We had friends in common; he knew my writing. He was extremely witty, almost to the point of being rude — but I took it as a challenge. We chatted in real time about work — he's a doctor — restaurants, our recent breakups and why the English, like himself, are into spanking. Amazing how the subject had turned to sex, and S/M in particular. He said he shied away from sexually submissive women these days. He felt they often wanted to be dominated for all the wrong reasons: emotionally damaged women who craved erotic humiliation to prove their own worthlessness.

"Maybe now's the time to get over your shyness," I typed.

"Maybe it is."

"Maybe you should give me your phone number." Better that I call him, in case he's a psychopath masquerading as a normal person.

At 11:30 P.M. West Coast time, I was lying naked on my bed, phone locked against my left shoulder, right hand poised. "How about a story?" I suggested.

"Let me think for a moment," he said. His voice was low and sexy and oh man, that British accent. He told me something that went like this:

"You're on a lonely road, somewhere in the Southwest, in the desert. You're hitchhiking and a green Citroën pulls up in a cloud of dust. Inside are two Mexican soap opera stars, a man and a woman. They pick you up, offer you some tequila and orange juice. You're drinking and driving fast and having fun when suddenly the car stops. There's a large boulder in

* Not his real name.

the middle of the road. The man gets out to investigate, while you and his girlfriend get out to stretch your legs. From behind the boulder steps a gorgeous outlaw cowgirl and soon it's evident that you're all being held up at gunpoint.

"The outlaw handcuffs the man and the woman, with their hands behind their back. She handcuffs you, too, with your hands in front. The outlaw thinks about robbing you all, but realizes there isn't anything to take. So she decides she wants something else. She wants to see something she could never see on TV. . . ."

I can't remember exactly how the story ended because I was coming so hard.

When I said, "How about a story?" I thought it was going to be one of those "and now I'm stroking your hair and running my hand up your thigh" blow-by-blow descriptions. Instead, it was like an episode of *Masterpiece Theatre* where everybody is suddenly ordered to participate in the most colossal daisy-chain perversities. The story was so beautiful and so dirty, it left me enormously satisfied and automatically guilty. When it was over, I blurted out, "If you tell anyone what we just did, I'll never speak to you again!" I felt so uncontrollably *Catholic.* I shouldn't have had cybersex on the first date. Big sin. I should have waited. It would have meant more if I'd waited!

The next morning, I replayed the evening's events in my head. Everything was great until I got to the part where I told him not to tell. How stupid. *Why* did I say that? Because I didn't trust him. What if he wrote things online about our liaison, the same way people write things on the bathroom wall? I didn't want to be what he expected — just another whore in cyberspace. I wanted to tell him how extraordinary our exchange had been for me, how rare. But it seemed much too soon to spell out the crazy, love-like feelings that were already taking over. I didn't want to come off as clingy, too relationshipy. If only he were lying next to me and could see the look in my eyes, feel the sincerity in my touch, I wouldn't have to say anything. Instead, "Don't tell!" fell out of my mouth. It was my childish, convoluted way of anointing our connection.

The next day, I apologized for my rude directive. Stephen sent me this bit of E-mail in return.

SUBJECT: Cab Fare's on the Table
REPLY from Stephen Hadley
24-SEP-93 16:18
I like that you are a Catholic. I like that you have done what you have done and can still feel guilt. That was one of my deepest fears, that everything that tastes forbidden to me now will one day be acceptable, and the frisson of transgression will be gone. Once the guilt and shame are gone, there's nothing but meat. Kind of.

I was now logging on to ECHO every twenty minutes, breathlessly anticipating our next communication. Telnet, log-in ID, password — come on, you stupid slow thing. New mail? Heart-stopping exhilaration. No mail? Crushing disappointment. I typed the O command, to see if he was online right now. Yes? I accidentally on purpose joined the conference he was in. No? I hung out, waiting. Reading through his old posts, trolling for background.

How could I be in so deep so fast, without any physical contact? Without even seeing what he looked like? Because from the moment I logged on and the words I longed to hear scrolled across my screen — smart, funny, doctor, English, top — I started to assemble my perfect lover. It happened subconsciously, against my better judgment.

In the real world, physical attraction is the catalyst that draws us in: If the body appeals to us, then we investigate sexual interests. But in the virtual world this process works in reverse: If our sexual interests match up, then we ask to see the body. As a result, there's an unprecedented openness in cyberspace. Disembodiment, ironically, leads to an immediately greater sense of intimacy. All the I-have-a-crush-on-you awkwardness that in real life gets padded by random three-dimensional distractions, like playing with the tiny sword that stabs your cocktail olive, must now be softened with words or the screen goes blank. All the thoughts that could otherwise be communicated with a look or a touch can now be conveyed only with the alphabet.

Telephone calls and in-person conversations are ephemeral. Spoken words vanish into thin air. Online communication leaves marks. Every chat can be saved on your hard drive for you to read over and over and over, to obsess about, analyze, strategically plan your next perfect string of vowels and consonants and spend hours wondering if it's all too good to be true. I laugh when I hear, "Online sex is safe sex! It's risk-free!" From disease, sure. But who's ever safe from the emotional stranglehold of love? Or heartbreak and jealousy?

Within a single day, Stephen and I easily exchanged fifty

messages. It wasn't just the volume of the responses that made it seem like things were happening so fast, but the rate of disclosure. In the absence of our physical bodies, the desire to know each other's minds became overwhelmingly urgent. I found myself confessing the most private truths about love, death, sex, religion, my family — all in the first twenty-four hours. Even for a loudmouth like me, it would have taken so much longer to coordinate the right place with the right time and the nerve to speak such things while looking into someone's eyes. I've heard a few true stories about so-called cyber cads — people swapping genders, switching tax brackets, lying about their age — who get their kicks from manipulating the guileless and lovelorn. But for most people I know, developing online love relationships is about being dead honest. And the truth, as we know, is often stranger than fiction.

In a spirited moment, I called up Susie and told her, "I'm having the greatest sex of my life and I've never even seen this guy!" She, along with everyone else, wondered, "How can that be?"

Stephen and I pushed our psychological and emotional boundaries to the edge because without our bodies, there was nothing else to push against. And it's the power of emotion and imagination that turns cybersex into *real* sex. Our conversations, electronic or otherwise, weren't less real or less meaningful to me because he wasn't lying in my arms. Yes, technically it was my hand on my clit, but it was the sentient exchanges between us that took me to the mountaintop. There was nothing I couldn't tell him. I'd never felt so uninhibited and so protected at the same time. His sexual hunger matched mine. Surpassed it, in fact. Anywhere, anytime I might answer the telephone only to hear him say, "Undress." And I would because, well, that's what those crazy, tilt-a-whirl maiden days are for.

SUBJECT: Why You Love Rubber
REPLY from Stephen Hadley
25-SEP-93 1:19
I love what I know of you, and respect you highly for how you think. And I like your "unusual" qualities V. much, from what you've showed me about them. I think you are awfully sweet.

Seven days into our affair, I suggested a meeting. He was reluctant. I couldn't believe it. I got a sick feeling, wondering if I'd been tricked. How could he not want to know me in person? Maybe I was just another conquest. Maybe his name wasn't even Stephen. He'd already seen my picture in various magazines and knew I wasn't a total dog. But as far as his appearance, I didn't have a clue. "So, what do you look like?" I once asked after a marathon phone session and he just sighed into the receiver; his amplified breath telling me that a physical description of himself was irrelevant to the magic between us. I immediately felt stupid for even asking. This is cyberspace, baby. Looks don't matter. So I let it slide, getting bits of information from one of our mutual acquaintances instead. "He's a big guy, tall. Curly brown hair," my friend David told me. "Sometimes he wears glasses." I was afraid if I pushed the issue too far, he would go away. I didn't want to lose him.

In virtual life, we can disengage from our bodies and all that travels with them: vanity, insecurity, sexual chemistry. At times it can even feel as if we've transcended the corporeal world. Bodies? How superficial! It's who you are on the *inside* that counts. But I've found that, at some point, the desire for the physical becomes overwhelming. You want it to be real or you don't want it. And once you decide to carry that fragile virtual egg across the threshold of real life, there is no turning back.

"Why won't you see me?" I typed. "I need an answer."

SUBJECT: Well, since you ask . . .
MESSAGE from Stephen Hadley
30-SEP-93 22:04
OK, girl. Answers to your questions:
I don't want to meet you now because I hate the way I look right now. And the way that I look right now is transient. I'm overweight, I'm out of shape, and I hate it. I have lost quite a lot of weight and have a bit more to go. I have become addicted to the experience of mining myself out of my slovenly husk, watching the numbers on the scale slide down, tightening my belt another notch. It's what I am *about*.

I suspect that my own self-image is a key factor in derailing a number of relationships I have had. I don't understand how people can love me, how people can find me attractive. I mean, I *know* that they do, but I can't understand it or see how. I almost respect them less if they are attracted to me. . . .

If you met me, three different things might happen:
  1. You would be disappointed and lose interest.
  2. You would be indifferent.

3. You would be pleased and be more interested in me.

None of those options can help me. And you couldn't be indifferent. You must be able to sense how interested I am in you. We are, as you so neatly put it, "tangled and connected on a few levels," which means that our first meeting will have all manner of weird pressures on it, so indifference is really not an option for you. I'm serious about not meeting until I'm finished.

Over the telephone, I insisted I didn't care how much he weighed. He insisted that my acceptance of him would only "fuck with his resolve" to lose weight. He refused to see me until July 4, 1994, when he would be "finished."

"Oh, everybody thinks they're too fat," I cheerfully empathized, "including me."

"Lisa." He was concentrating so hard he could barely speak. "I'm working my way down from three hundred and fifty pounds."

In a subsequent correspondence, he wrote, "I DON'T WANT TO BE ACCEPTED AS I AM NOW. I don't want to be what I am now."

It was too late. I was in love. Stephen was the first man who accepted in me what so many others found unacceptable: my erotic determination. He accepted it unconditionally, 100 percent. He *got* me, my essence, in a way no one else ever had. All of the things I spent so much time explaining to other men — my ideas on pornography, feminism, sex — were perfectly clear to Stephen from the get-go. Where others tried to change me and make me feel ashamed of what I did and who

I was, Stephen told me my existence was like an amulet to him, warding off cruelty, violence, despair. He called me his hero.

• • •

My thirtieth birthday was coming up, and as a preparation for old age I went for a facial. There I was, reclining on a chaise lounge in the semidarkness under a soft blanket, listening to twinkly, ambient music. The clinician placed cool cotton pads over my eyes so I couldn't see a thing and began to slather my face with exfoliating goo. It was heavenly to lie there and be pampered, blind to the world around me, with one of Stephen's filthy stories going through my head. Then it hit me: What if I met Stephen without actually seeing him?

SUBJECT: Very Pretty
REPLY from Lisa Palac
02-OCT-93 12:37
I want you to see me. But I won't see you because I'll be blindfolded. I'm smiling now. . . .

REPLY from Stephen Hadley
02-OCT-93 16:42
Not as broadly as me, babe.

We made arrangements to meet at his New York City apartment on the evening of my birthday. Venus, a close friend of Stephen's and a friend of a friend of mine, whom he described as "stunningly beautiful and quite adventurous," would act as our liaison. Venus would greet me at the door and put a velvet blindfold over my eyes. She would only remove it after my visit with Stephen had ended.

The physical risks were the least of my worries. Stephen and I'd had the big talk about our sexual histories. We'd both gotten tested for HIV and knew how to operate latex. The idea that he might try to harm me — rape me or even kill me — crossed my mind under the subject heading Anything's Possible, but the chances of it actually happening were less than zero. No, to me the highest risks were the emotional ones. My greatest fear was that we would meet and it would be all wrong, and I'd be left wondering, How will my heart ever survive this?

In our last correspondence before our meeting, Stephen wrote:

> And so I close my eyes, and fold my hands and wait to meet you. Here, then, will be the moment when I must confront the possibility of my own death, the collision for me of the sexual and my possible extinction from your world. I have never felt so inadequate, so aware of my flaws, so conscious of things I *don't* have to offer. And the other women who have loved me and wanted me don't help me now, as it is only you I want to want me and only you who will know whether you want me or not. I'm not frightened, but calm. In fact, I don't know when I last felt so alive.

At 7:00 P.M. on November 4, I checked in with Stephen's doorman, walked through the long foyer and took the elevator up to the seventh floor. I knocked on apartment 7B. Venus answered, looking like Sharon Stone — only better. She was tall and muscled-up, with shoulder-length blond hair that felt like cashmere and a voice just as soft. She was wearing a black PVC corset and thong, and thigh-high, stiletto-heeled black boots. "Happy birthday," she said as she kissed my cheek. She took me by the hand and led me down the hall.

The front room of Hadley Manor was huge, with pale hardwood floors and one wall of windows that stretched to the ceiling, fourteen feet up. It was empty except for a futon covered in a white sheet, dozens of stargazer lilies and the light of thirty or so cathedral candles. Venus took my coat and handed me a glass of champagne. Then she blindfolded me and left me alone. I stood in the middle of the room, wearing a red plaid schoolgirl skirt, a white shirt and, as instructed, white cotton panties. It was perfectly quiet except for the roar of blood agitating in my skull, hurting my ears. And from my perspective, it was now completely dark.

I heard his shoes clicking on the floor. His hand touched my shoulder. I pressed my cheek against it.

"You're shaking," he said.

"I know," I replied. He took my glass and led me to the futon, where I lay down in his arms. He pressed up against me and stroked my hair for a long, long time, telling me sweet things until my ragged breaths were smooth. I tried to pay attention to his words, but his completeness was overwhelming. There was too much of him. Not in terms of his physical size but in the number of details: the smell of his breath as he talked, the thin layer of sweat on the palms of his hands, the fleshy softness of his belly, the way he was touching me. I assessed a few bits of critical, chemical information — *So this is what he smells like. What think? I think it's . . . sniffffffff . . . it's good* — and, thankfully, gave them high marks. We kissed and his fingers started to influence things under my skirt. Then I heard Venus walk back into the room, kneel down and begin to untie the laces of my shoes.

Until that night, I never truly believed my body was beautiful. Call it insecurity left over from when I was a four-eyed fat kid going through puberty; when my mother dutifully reminded me how far my right ear stuck out and how one day *we* would have it surgically tucked back. Insecurity exacerbated by a string of old boyfriends who told me I'd look better if I dropped a few pounds, if I did some sit-ups, had my tits lifted. But these two, they ooohed and aaahed with the utmost reverence over every little piece of me, seeing only perfection where I saw a blemish. Our scheduled evening of strict dominance quickly turned love fest. "Isn't she beautiful? Isn't she perfect?" they repeated like a prayer while they stroked and examined every part of me.

About five hours later, I asked if I could make a change in our plans.

"Can I take this off?" I said, touching my last sartorial remnant, the blindfold.

"Yes," Stephen said, without hesitation.

Simply to see after this kind of sensory deprivation put me in a state of amazing grace. Everything sparkled.

And to see what I had known only as an amorphous voice and a string of text materialize into a living, breathing human being with eyes that blinked and hands that reached out for me was really, really weird. It was hard for me to tear up the picture of Stephen I'd carried in my mind for so long, but I had to because it was wrong. Watching him speak and move was like watching a movie that kept going in and out of sync and focus. One moment his body was in total agreement with his personality. At last, it's you! How perfect. The next, it was fuzzy and surreal. Am I dreaming? Who *is* this person? Why does this familiar voice keep coming out of this unrecognizable mouth?

But to see, for the first time, after traveling three thousand miles, the face of the person I loved *after* we had made love rearranged my soul.

"So this is you," I said. Stephen still had all of his clothes on: a black cotton turtleneck, khakis. His smile was endless and I ran my finger over his teeth, lingering on the chip in his front tooth. I held his hand and examined the shape of his fingernails, tears slipping down my cheeks. I watched his hips sway as he walked into the kitchen to get my birthday cake and thought, *You are so beautiful.*

6

Spiritualized

"**NOW THAT I'VE FOUND** happiness, all I do is worry about losing it. Am I nuts or what?"

Six months into a pretty great relationship with Stephen, I was sitting in my shrink's office, wondering out loud if a healthy, long-term love was even in the cards. I started therapy right after Ron and I split up, in an effort to understand why I almost married Mr. Wrong, why I still felt responsible for my mother's chronic depression and why I was so often compelled to please the people who hurt me. I was making great progress. After seven issues I'd handed in my resignation at *Future Sex,* thrilled at the prospect of giving up the fight for editorial control. Unemployment never felt so good! My business dealings with Ron were going smoothly, and I was in love again. I was on top of the world. Which meant there was nowhere to go but down.

"That's the Catholic doctrine talking," my therapist insisted. A wise woman in her early sixties, she believed that my anxiety stemmed from a religious idea that happiness comes only to those who suffer for it.

"How do you know it's not just run-of-the-mill paranoia? I'll bet there are millions of happy people who feel like the rug is going to be yanked out from under them any second now!"

"Yes, but only one of them is named Lisa Palac. You're living your life according to principles you've never closely examined," she explained. "You need to look at the doctrine."

Right. I spent fourteen years looking at the stupid doctrine. I knew all there was to know about being Catholic and I had rejected it all.

My distrust of the system began in first grade when we learned that everyone who wasn't Catholic was going to hell because they were not part of our one, true religion. I never believed that if you died wearing a scapula (basically a string with two tiny holy cards attached to it) you'd go straight to heaven, that innocent babies were all born with Original Sin, that the Pope was infallible or that the little white wafer I received on my tongue during Holy Communion was the actual body of Jesus Christ. More important, I was never able to reconcile the unconditionally loving God with the one who demanded brutal, painful tests of love. Eventually, since I'd never been much of a believer in the first place, the logical extension was to excommunicate myself.

One summer when I returned home from college I told my mother I wasn't Catholic anymore. She wouldn't have any of it.

"You can never *not* be Catholic! You were baptized! What about your communion? Your confirmation?" She hhhmphed.

"Not Catholic." She rolled her eyes and patted the back of her tall hairdo. "Please."

She was right.

For years, whenever I mentioned that I was raised Catholic someone would inevitably holler, "Well *that* explains everything!" But to me, it explained very little. I knew all about the reputation of Catholic girls (naughty little sluts who vented their taboo desires in the most intense and obscure ways) and I'd heard all the jokes (constant maneuvering around the land mines of sin is an exhausting way to live, but Jesus Christ, the sex is incredible!) and I'd be the first to concede some truth to the stereotype — whatever's prohibited becomes tremendously appealing. But the catalyst for my professional interest in sex was feminist politics, not the Stations of the Cross. Yes, I had certainly performed more than a few acts of contrition around sex — but who hadn't? Catholics certainly don't corner the market on shame, guilt or desire for the forbidden.

But now I was beginning to realize that my big intellectual dismissal of the Church had done little to loosen its emotional grip on me. The very fact that I was so unwilling to turn around and confront its teachings was such an obvious sign that Catholicism was still dogging me. Honestly? I was scared to look back, scared of becoming a believer. My mother's words haunted me: "Millions of people can't be wrong!" At the very least, I knew how upset I'd get, having to read all the rules for salvation that I hated reading the first time around. Yet I knew I had to do it. A spiritual showdown was not only inevitable but necessary if I expected to evolve as a human being. But instead of sticking my nose in a catechism book like I was supposed to, I walked into Tower Records and bought *Jesus Christ Superstar,* the double CD set.

In the early seventies, my entire family went to see *Jesus Christ Superstar,* a rock opera chronicling the last week of Christ's life, from his donkey ride into Jerusalem to his crucifixion. Getting high on Jesus was definitely the most countercultural thing going on in my neighborhood, trickling down diluted into our middle-class Chicago section of "straight" establishment long after the original, long-haired Jesus freaks had left their California communes. I saw the pop musical *Godspell,* where Jesus and his disciples all dressed like clowns, and I knew every song on the album. At guitar Mass on Sundays, I sang Sister Janet Mead's rockin' version of "The Lord's Prayer" (number four on the *Billboard* chart) and George Harrison's "My Sweet Lord." These tiny doses of experiential Christianity were my only memories of a good connection to the Church; of feeling something other than frightened or bored.

In times of great confusion, I always put on a favorite record looking for hope, solace, an explanation, maybe even a vision. Now I was counting on *Superstar* to work some juju on me. I thought if I listened to the lyrics carefully, I might gain some insight into this connection between happiness and suffering.

As soon as I hit play, I was dancing around the room, singing along with Judas (*Did you mean to die like that? Was that a mistake or/Did you know your messy death would be a record-breaker?*) and belting it out with Mary Magdalene (*I don't know how to LOVE him*). The skeptic and the sensualist definitely have the best numbers in the show. Suddenly an old sound bite slipped into my head from — where? *American Bandstand? It's got a funky beat and you can dance to it.* And I realized the reason I felt such a positive connection to *Superstar* so many years ago was not because it was a moving story about Jesus but because the music *physically* moved me. It's the reason I've always been a rock fan, even before I could read the lyrics, much less understand them: rock allowed me the pleasure of my body. In the music I found the fervor, the rapturous communion, the transformation from body to a bodiless place, the kinds of revelations that I was supposed to find in church. I have religious experiences with everything except religion. The religion I got was all about denial of the body: denying it food, beauty, denying it physical pleasure of all kinds. (This is why Catholic hymns are so dull. Because you're not supposed to move anywhere below your neck — that would be sinful.) The spirit and the intellect were presented as superior and good, the physical as inferior and evil. The bottom line was this: The more sexual you are, the less moral you are. Yet I've found so much truth in sex, and some of my deepest spiritual experiences have also been sexual ones.

Like a lot of people I know, my spiritual experiences take place well beyond the walls of organized religion. They tend to spring up out of an intensely physical act and, so far, they've happened quite by accident, too: the "I'm gonna die out here!" kind of exhaustion on a wilderness trek, the time I had my labia pierced, the sensation of having a man's entire hand inside my vagina. I never start out seeking The Truth, I'm just in it for the adventure, for the physical pleasure and then, whoa! it hits me. I am so deep inside my body that I am, simultaneously, outside of it. I'm struck by how trivial I am in the big universe picture and how significant I am at the same time. My ego? Gone. I surrender. And I feel like I've got another piece of the Life and Death puzzle, even though it might be a very, very small piece.

To be fair, the Catholic tradition does include the body as a vehicle for out-of-body spiritual transformation. It boasts an assortment of saints whose peak experiences include flipping into catatonic trances, levitating, developing stigmata, going blind, getting shot full of arrows and all-around virgin martyrdom. In paintings and on holy cards, the expression on these saints' faces is one of ecstasy, while their bloody bodies carry proof that they have been personally touched by the Holy Spirit. Christ on the cross is the supreme example. Always depicted as a beautiful man, he hangs dying, nearly naked, radiating sensuality. The physical experience of sex was, of course, conveniently excluded from this divine path, but the message that physical trials — especially very painful ones — can lead to ecstatic spiritual heights wasn't lost on me. It stuck with me, even long after I'd left the Church in the dust.

• • •

Inching closer to the inevitable, my next step was to rent a film I'd always wanted to see, Martin Scorsese's *Last Temptation of Christ.* In it, Jesus accepts an angel's last-minute offer to be taken down from the cross and trades being the Messiah for sex with Mary Magdalene and life as an ordinary man. With music by Peter Gabriel, it features an all-star cast including David Bowie (Pontius Pilate), Harvey Keitel (Judas) and Willem Dafoe as Jesus, the carpenter who builds crosses for killing Jews. Released in 1988, the film was boycotted by censor king Reverend Donald Wildmon and his American Family Association for its all-too-human portrayal of Jesus, which, fortunately, resulted in scads of publicity for the film.

The opening scene has Jesus delivering a cross to a scheduled crucifixion. When Jesus and the Romans finally nail the convicted criminal to the cross, they strip him of all of his clothing and he is totally naked. Later in the film, Jesus is also crucified naked. Now, I already knew that Jesus was stripped of his clothes before his crucifixion because it's the tenth Station of the Cross, with the twelfth Station being "And He died naked on the Cross." But every image of the crucifixion I've ever seen has shown Jesus with a slip of white cloth below his hips. So, was he naked or not? A small but critical detail. A detail which I'd been fixated on since I was old enough to read. A detail I'd guilt-tripped myself for even *thinking*. Naked Jesus — how blasphemous. But just imagine for a moment what the world would be like if on every crucifix in the world, in every cathedral, interpreted by every painter and every sculptor and hanging over every bed, there He was, naked and unashamed.

The morning after *Last Temptation,* my friend David Pescovitz called to see what was up. I told him I was researching the history of crucifixion.

"Like, as some kinky sex thing?"

"No!" I snorted. "As some Roman death thing." I went on to tell him he'd lived in San Francisco too long. That's when he told me about Club Jesus, a Sunday night dance spot where they allegedly nailed some pierced and tattooed Modern Primitive guy up on a cross as an erotic performance piece.

"No!" My mouth hung open in disbelief — but only for a second. I flashed back to an art history class I'd taken in college when we learned about a performance artist named Chris Burden who, in 1974, nailed himself to a Volkswagen Beetle. And so the tradition continues.

While I've never nailed myself to anything, I certainly understand the desire to take the dramatic, religious rituals and symbols once considered inviolable — that once had power over me — and rewrite their significance in my favor. For years I despised my Catholic school uniform as a paean to blind allegiance and conformity. When schoolgirl chic hit the early 1990s, however, I was the first in line for a little plaid skirt. Suddenly, the object of my derision had become an aphrodisiac: I found the uniform look incredibly erotic. I was attracted to the very things about it that once repelled me — its representation of willingness, obedience and innocence — especially since I'd known the pleasures of being unwilling, disobedient and aware. Schoolgirl uniforms as fetish wear, rosaries as jewelry, confessional booths at leather clubs, crucifixion as art — they're more than trendy, they're an appropriation of power.

Anyway, my search for historical facts on crucifixion proved successful. I discovered it was common practice to crucify people naked, adding extra humiliation to the already disgraceful spectacle of public execution. And it got me thinking: If they were covering up the reality of His crucifixion, what else was a lie? I'd always assumed the whole "sex is sinful" philosophy was based on something Jesus said. But maybe I was wrong. Maybe the Church had taken Christ's views on sexuality and twisted them around to promote some prudish pope's sex-hating agenda. Maybe Jesus was a sex-positive guy after all.

I decided to play biblical scholar and read everything Jesus ever said about sex. I didn't get very far. In the Gospels of Matthew, Mark, Luke and John, Jesus has virtually nothing to say about sex. How could this be? I turned to the works of theological experts — Elaine Pagels, E. P. Sanders, John Dominic Crossan — looking for an explanation, but they only made my head spin faster. I learned that Christ himself never wrote down a single word. That Matthew, Mark, Luke and John weren't four *actual* men but four anonymous groups of people who wrote things down sixty to one hundred years after Christ's death. That there are many other gospels that never made it into the canon, such as the Gospel of Thomas, of Philip, of Truth. In Elaine Pagel's book, *Adam, Eve and the Serpent,* she discusses the man who so tremendously influenced our sexual attitudes:

> Augustine, one of the greatest teachers of western Christianity, derived many of these attitudes from the story of Adam and Eve: that sexual desire is sinful; that infants are infected from the moment of conception with the disease of original sin; and that Adam's sin corrupted the whole of nature itself.

People often ask me what I find shocking, assuming it'll be some kind of gross sex act. But if there's one thing I've been truly shocked by in my life it's this: ignorance of my own faith after fourteen years of Catholic education. I was a bright student, got good grades. I excelled at memorize and repeat, and can still recite an entire Mass by heart. But the Bible? Never read much of it. Catholics, I hear, rarely do.

After this dramatic discovery, there were long slots of time where I did nothing but sit still and listen to the high-pitched voice of ridicule inside my head: *How could you not know that? You are so stupid.* Between the episodes of self-torture, however, came the realization that it was time to seriously take my shrink up on her offer.

• • •

My therapist lent me a book, *The New Saint Joseph Baltimore Catechism.* Published in 1964, it contains the teachings I learned as a schoolgirl. The illustrations are done in black and white and red, and consist almost entirely of pictures of Jesus, lambs and blood. The front cover shows handsome Jesus holding a lamb, like one would hold a newborn baby. The back cover features a drawing of a bloody Christ on the cross and the Virgin Mary gazing up at him, her hands folded in prayer. Setting up its audience for plenty of chills and thrills, the text reads:

SEE His bleeding wounds.
SEE the nails in His hands and feet.
SEE the thorns in his head.
SEE His side open for us to enter.
SEE how much He loves us.
HOW do you think our Lady felt?
HOW should we feel?
If Jesus loves us so much, what are we going to do for Him today?

The book is divided into lessons like "The Purpose of Man's Existence," "Actual Sin" and "How to Make a Good Confession." Each lesson offers a few verses from the Bible, and then a long interpretation of the verses by the Catholic authorities, followed by a quiz. For example, when we're introduced to the section on Genesis titled "Creation and the Fall of Man," the myth is explained like this: "The devil tempted Eve first and she led Adam into sin. They chose the forbidden fruit. This means they chose to please themselves instead of God. This was the first or ORIGINAL sin." Adam and Eve were selfish, selfish, selfish! Underneath this explanation of Adam and Eve's decision to eat of the Tree of Knowledge of Good and Evil is a black box containing an exercise: "Practice: Please God even when this means doing something hard."

Frankly, I can't read the story of Adam and Eve without getting totally pissed off. Before we even get to the Apple Incident, the details of Eve's creation are up in the air. Genesis, chapter 1, verse 27: "So God created man in his own image, in the image of God he created him; male and female he created them." Okay, fine. But in chapter 2 God suddenly makes them again, this time creating Adam from dust and Eve from Adam's rib. And Eve is called "Woman, because she was taken out of man." What an absurd piece of revisionist propaganda — the whole bit about woman being flesh of *his* flesh. Everybody knows it's the other way around.

Sometimes I wonder what the world would be like if the Bible said, "And Eve ate the apple and her eyes were opened to the mysterious beauty and violence of life. She gave some to Adam who fell to his knees with gratitude, thanking her for taking the veil of unawareness from him. And they saw what a bore innocence was, sitting around all day with nothing to do." And I start plotting out what Adam and Eve did or didn't do in their fictional paradise. I once wrote a story where I made Eve into a courageous heroine who was out have interesting conversations with snakes while Adam was being a layabout blockhead. I thought that if I could just spin the story, I could feel good about it. But I can't. I can't accept it and I can't rewrite it and I can't throw it away.

The catechism book is obsessed with the sin of selfishness. Next to the Original Sin quiz is a drawing of two little girls fighting over a doll with the caption, "We are all born selfish."

In another, two boys look out the window at the rain, holding their baseball mitts.

"Too bad it's raining."

"When we accept things like this from God without complaining, it helps to clean the selfishness out of our soul."

The doctrine offers other equally bizarre (and grammatically confusing) methods of ridding ourselves of the evil that makes us dirty and unfit for the kingdom of heaven, such as "We die to ourselves each time we do something we don't feel like doing to please Him. This kills the selfishness in us" and "In Baptism we promise to live our lives for the love of God in imitation of Christ, and not for the love of ourselves in imitation of the devil." Selfishness has always been my Achilles' heel. Selfish was the worst thing someone could call me, and now I knew why.

However, the overarching lesson to be learned here is not that selfishness lies at the root of all sin but that *suffering is love*. A quiz asks, "What do we learn from the sufferings and death of Christ? The suffering and death of Christ show us how much God loves man." Over and over this theme repeats itself. Later, these instructions pop up: "Be obedient for the love of Jesus, especially when it is hard" and "Look at a crucifix each day and think how much Jesus suffered for our sins."

Reading along I often had to stop, so angry I couldn't focus. Sunken childhood memories floated to the surface. I remembered how sick to my stomach I used to feel every time I refused to greet hardships and unfair demands with beatific acceptance, every time I took a shot at self-preservation and independence. I didn't want to be a selfish, sinning loveless bad person, yet what was the alternative? Guilt. To consider my own needs in any way was selfish and therefore a sin, and when I sinned I felt guilty, which of course led me back to suffering. It was a sick cycle where *not* suffering was basically impossible.

One look at my own journal entries shows me that I recognize the value in suffering. When my life is a mess I scribble furiously, trying to make sense of all my pain and accrue some wisdom from it. But here's the clincher: If suffering is love, then *not* suffering is *not* love. If the only true love is the love of God, which can only be truly demonstrated through suffering, then there's no room for joy. There's no place for real love and happiness in our relationships to ourselves, with others and the world around us.

With great clarity I began to see the flaw in the logic of suffering for love and how this defective reasoning continued to govern my life. I was unhappy because I'd been trained to believe that happiness is spiritually inferior to suffering; that only the insights I acquire through pain are valid and authentic. On some unconscious level, I perpetuated unfulfilling relationships because I accepted suffering as the *only* route to love. Conversely, when I found myself in a warm, fulfilling relationship, I feared losing it — because I wasn't suffering. Armed with this new truth, I very consciously set out to change my approach to love and happiness.

Oh, but there was one tiny snag. In the process of discovering how tenaciously I'd embraced the concept of suffering for love, I also discovered how intensely I'd eroticized it. Please me, love me, obey me even when it's painful — these were the words I longed to hear in bed. *You'll do it to please me, even though it's hard? Show me how much you love me. Be a good girl for Daddy.* So. How was I going to rid myself of the despair caused by this fucked-up doctrine without losing the hot sexual fantasies it inspired?

• • •

In general, my sexual fantasies have always revolved around this theme: I'm a grown woman who gets to act like a little girl. I am wide-eyed, innocent and oh-so-willing, in that Lolita kind of way. I get punished for being naughty, rewarded for being good and, heaven knows, I aim to please. But the faceless authoritarian in my erotic imagination never had a name until the day an unsolicited piece of lesbian fiction arrived at the *On Our Backs* office. Titled "Daddy's Little Girl" by Ann Wertheim, it begins:

> My daddy comes into my bedroom late at night. She puts her hand under the blanket and up my nightgown and pushes her finger roughly up my pussy hole and whispers, "Daddy wants to fuck her little girl. Shhh, you're wet already, you need this, don't you, that's a girl, good girl. Daddy's going to fuck her little pussy girl with her hard cock. That's what you want, isn't it?"

The story sent everyone at the office into a tailspin. We all found it both disturbing and incredibly arousing. I was particularly hung up on two questions: How could a lesbian be a daddy? and How *dare* I get off on it? Daddy was definitely the name of the masculine persona dishing out the love and erotic punishment in my fantasy — I just never had the guts to say it.

We decided to publish the story but felt the need to address the concerns — even outrage — that a story like this would raise. In the same issue, fiction editor Marcy Sheiner wrote an essay titled "The Daddy Closet" and stated it's the *gestalt* of Daddy — strong, provider, protector — not our real fathers that makes scenes like this erotic. Daddy is a benevolent dictator who loves but also punishes. Daddy is not necessarily a man but rather "an omnipotent lover who will stick with us through the pain." Likewise, Little Girl is not an actual child but the essence of vulnerability, innocence and trust. She isn't always little and she isn't always a biological girl and, most important, she isn't always good, otherwise the game would be no fun.

Despite Marcy's valid explanation that Daddy fantasies don't necessarily represent sexual desire for our real fathers, I couldn't help thinking they were connected. How could they not be? If sexual fantasies are an adult way of dealing with the conflicts experienced during our formative years, then Daddy, either by his presence or his absence, figures into that mix. My own Daddy fantasy was no doubt linked to conflicts I experienced with my own father, and represented a continued longing for the love and approval that I alternately did and didn't get as a child. After all, I'm an Original Daddy's Girl who spent hours on her father's lap being extra-cute and gingerly stringing out her demands until he'd laugh and say, "Whatever my little peanut wants." But it wasn't until I picked up that catechism book years later that I got to the bottom of it all.

At its core, my Daddy fantasy isn't about my father but about Our Father Who Art in Heaven. I'd taken the dynamic of love and punishment, which terrorized me as a child and made me feel helpless — kneeling down and sticking out my tongue to receive his body, whispering my most sinful transgressions in a dark confessional, doing penance to show my love — and turned it into a powerful source of erotic pleasure. It wasn't a conscious decision, but then, sexual fantasies rarely are.

Granted, it seems weird to eroticize something that's troubling. But the fact is, where there's conflict, there's excitement. Man versus man, nature, the cosmos, himself — every good story needs conflict, including the sexual stories we script for ourselves. And while it would seem that once the conflict is resolved the story's over, not all stories have clean-cut endings. Despite my fear that all of my intellectual processing would ruin my best sexual fantasy, it didn't. It's still a turn-on because I'm *still* struggling with the after-effects of Catholicism and I always will be. The Church so broadly and indelibly shaped my identity, only my parents can top its influence.

A friend recently asked me, "If you had it to do all over again, would you want to be raised Catholic?" Strangely, I found myself saying yes. Although I wouldn't wish it on anyone else, I am grateful, in a way, for my indoctrination. It's certainly given me a keen understanding and appreciation for things like power, high drama and ritual. Not to mention plastic Jesus nite-lights, novena candles and shrines to Our Lady of Guadalupe. While I've rejected the official meaning of all the Catholic icons, I'm still undeniably attached to them in the same way that you can never be unrelated to your family. They symbolize my cultural past, they're part of where I come from, just like the Chicago Cubs or Polish sausage.

And while I will never respect this faith that refused to acknowledge the sexual as the spiritual, I now realize that I'll never be completely free of it either. My tears, my marks, the look of ecstasy on my face, the taste of sex in my mouth, this is my proof that I have been touched by the spirit.

7

Degrade Me When I Ask You To

ONE NIGHT I WAS having dinner with my friend Matisse, unloading my latest theories on dominance and submission. "I *never* would have picked you for a bottom," he said with a laugh.

"Well, you can't tell by looking," I replied.

Until February 1994, to be exact, the only people who knew my intimate interests were a few lovers, my shrink and a couple of close friends. I wasn't neurotically private about it, I wasn't ashamed of it, there just weren't many occasions to make public announcements about it. I wasn't into leather, I didn't have a scene and, after all, I was living in San Francisco, a city where fistfucking demonstrations had become ho-hum and people stuck nails through their dicks as nightclub entertainment. Erotic discipline? Big whoop. Then *Esquire* magazine ran an article with the headline "YES. That's the message from a new generation of women thinkers, who are embracing sex (and men!). Call them 'do me' feminists. But can they save the penis from the grassy field of American history?" (*Can we save the penis from the grassy field of American history? What does that mean?* I imagine a group of Florence Nightingale types with crisp white hats and lamps, wandering a hillside in some smoky Civil War scene and picking up tiny severed penises.)

The article was a compilation of interviews with me, Susie Bright, Naomi Wolf, bell hooks, Katie Roiphe, Mary Gaitskill, Rene Denfeld and Rebecca Walker — all of us supposedly supercharged sexy feminist sluts who liked to screw men! Sure, the article was a celebration of female sexual power but wrapped in the wild applause was another point: Dear *Esquire* readers: There are still women out there who will fuck you, even if they call themselves feminists. Don't worry.

My picture is featured on the opening page. In it, I am wearing nothing but a sleeping bag. I am standing barefoot in the woods, smiling. Underneath the photo runs this caption:

"I say to men, 'Okay, pretend you're a burglar and you've broken in here and you throw me down on the bed and make me suck your cock!' They're horrified — it goes against all they've been taught: 'No, no, it would degrade you!' Exactly. Degrade me when I ask you to."

Now the cat was out of the bag. Lisa Palac: writer, feminist and submissive cocksucker. To be sexually submissive and Catholic is perfectly understandable — with its merciless doctrine of pain, punishment and redemption, the Catholic church is the biggest S/M community in the world. But to be sexually submissive and a *feminist?* Incomprehensible. Suddenly everyone wanted to know: How can you be a feminist and be on the bottom? I'd laugh and say, "Because everyone is fighting to be on the bottom!" And I wasn't being totally insincere. In the S/M community, submissives outnumber dominants 100 to 1, with men wanting to be sexually dominated just as much as — if not more than — women do. Yet even outside the scene, most people in their own secret way like to give up erotic control, to be swept away and be the center of attention.

It's fairly easy to admit, even among the most humble, a longing to be the first, the best, the top. America is built on competition and winning. It's much more difficult to admit a longing for surrender. Acquiescence is seen as giving in, losing, which is exactly the thing we're told not to want. I have plenty of dominant fantasies and I can sure dish it out, but being on top isn't the problem — it's what's expected. I am *supposed* to be walking all over men's faces in my high heels — not kneeling down and worshipping their cocks.

When a woman asks me, "How can you be a feminist and a bottom?" it's often because she's in the same boat and she wants to know how the hell it could happen. In hushed voices, women have told me what they want: to be called names — whore, slut. To be made to crawl for it. To take it until it hurts, until the tears come. Not all the time, but sometimes. Yeah, I say, me too. They're relieved. Safety in numbers. Still, how can an independent, strong-willed feminist enjoy being degraded and humiliated during sex? It's these words — *degraded* and *humiliated* — that set off the alarm. It's one thing to want a few love bites, a good hard fuck, even a light spanking or some silk scarf bondage. But why would a woman choose to be sexually humiliated — especially by a man — if she wasn't psychologically damaged in some way?

First, the idea that feminists are supposed to have egalitarian sexual fantasies or sex lives is ridiculous. Do the sexual lives of Democrats or Republicans jibe with their politics? Let's be serious. Fantasy is what our imagination does because it can. Fantasy takes the mind where the body cannot or will not go, and the human imagination travels from the sublime to the contemptible whether we like it or not. Second, outside the context of an orchestrated sexual scene, who wants to be forced to do anything? But in context, the rules change.

When people say they're "into" S/M, it's like saying they're into food. It begs the questions: What kind? How often? How much? S/M usually brings to mind sexual encounters where one person inflicts physical pain upon another, but it also describes scenes of intense psychological control where pain takes a backseat. If you think of S/M as one of those X-Y graphs, where X is the vertical sadistic/masochistic vector — the pain scale — and Y is the horizontal dominant/submissive vector — the mind scale — the infinite combinations of psychological and physical control become more obvious. Some people want to play with really intense sensations of pain — whipping, cutting, clothespins — without any humiliation. Some are into the head games more than anything else and want to be made to do exactly as they're told with little or no physical pain. Me? I've always scored low on the pain scale, and high on the mind scale. And you? We all have our place on this graph, you know.

Nevertheless, the most popular S/M question is Why pain? Because it hurts so good. Physiologically, when our body experiences pain it releases natural painkillers called endorphins that put us in a blissed-out, tranquil state. When we're sexually aroused our sensitivity to pain decreases, as it does whenever our blood starts pumping because we're feeling angry, afraid or simply athletic. (Funny how "No pain, no gain" is the athlete's motto, yet we don't make the kind of moral judgments about sports that we do about sex.) Likewise, if we're stressed-out, upset or in some other fragile mood, our sensitivity to pain increases.

But the truth is, I've never been attracted to S/M for the endorphin rush. The question Why head games? isn't answered by physiology. Catholicism is one explanation for my submissive desires, but certainly not the only one. Why do I want what I want?

- Because women are supposed to be desired, not do the desiring. If I am "forced" to do all sorts of filthy things in bed — the things I secretly want to do — it's a way for me to be an absolute whore without having to take responsibility for it.
- Because danger is exciting. I love the sensation of being a little bit frightened, very aroused and safe from any real harm.
- Because power is one of the greatest aphrodisiacs. When I submit to my lover, I feel incredibly powerful. Paradoxical, but true. When I willingly relinquish control it's an act of strength, not weakness. I gauge my power — and my erotic pride — by how much I can take, how much attention I command and how good I am at getting what I want.
- Because chances are, it's genetic. Perhaps my sexual proclivities, along with my pug nose and poor eyesight,

have been passed on from generation to generation. Do I get it from my mother's side? My father's side? Who else in my family is like me?

• Because sex by nature is aggressive, even deadly. Anyone who's ever watched a *National Geographic* special knows that when animals mate, it's rarely gentle and pretty. Being part of the animal kingdom, I'm no exception.

• Because all women who have submissive desires are eroticizing their oppression. It doesn't matter if the players are dykes — it's not like lesbians missed out on all those centuries of patriarchal subjugation. Thirty years of feminism can't undo the legacy of male privilege or erase the fact that civilizations were built on the idea that women are nothing but pieces of property, and the gender war is far from over. S/M is my choice. Of my own free will, I have made the decision to engage in it as an equal. But maybe the reason why I chose it in the first place is because it's a way for me to get pleasure out of the shitty, second-class social hand I've been dealt. When you've got a lemon, make lemonade.

• Because I eroticize hostility, fear, guilt and anger. *Because I eroticize everything.* I take the ups and downs, the pain, the pleasure and use it all to my sexual advantage.

I grew up believing that sex lives high above the shadows, glowing, white and sacred. Unlike the rest of my life, with its constellations of anxiety and rage and ambivalence, my sex life was supposed to be safely contained in a sphere of cozy feel-goodness. Granted, I was also taught to contain my black and blue emotions. When I was angry, I was told to calm down.

When I was sad, I was encouraged to cheer up. The one thing I was never told was to stop acting so goddamn happy. Yes, there was a time and a place for hostility, but it certainly wasn't when I had my legs spread.

Well into adulthood, I still clung to the belief that once I crawled out from under the wet blanket of guilt and shame and political correctness, I would feel completely at ease with, and self-affirmed by, every fantasy that popped into my head and everything I did in bed. Once I understood the pleasure, the emotional truths and especially the divine benefits of sex, sex would never be troubling again. Was I wrong. I've worked hard to reconcile my politics with my sexuality but they rarely fit together, all nice and neat. If they did, life would be easy. Sex is right up there with love and death and truth — raging with contradiction.

Despite all of my critical thinking about S/M, guilt and ambivalence still make regular appearances. I can say that gender is a construct or that my partner and I *exchange sexual power* (a popular definition of S/M) but when a man slaps my face — no matter how much I want him to do it and no matter how hot it makes me or how much I love him — he is still a man slapping my face. And in darker moments, I say to myself: How can I allow it? Especially in light of all the crimes committed by Men, the monolith?

Men and their historical hatred of women, from Eve on down. Men and their sexual jealousy and possessiveness, their violent history of raping and beating and killing the women they say they love. Men pressing up against me on a crowded bus, stealthily grinding their hard-ons into my ass. Men making me feel afraid, helpless. Sometimes I get in these moods where I begin to tally up Men's violations and the Man-Hater in me rises to the surface. Eye for an eye. I have visions of how I'll deal with the next asshole who gets in my way — or my sister's way. Of how I'll make him kneel down and beg to suck the barrel of my .45 before I blow his fucking head off.

Yet those Men are not my lovers. My lovers know me and I know them, we aren't strangers. They've held me when I was sick, encouraged me when I was despondent, made me laugh, treated me with respect and kindness. And if we made the kind of powerful sexual connection where tenderness merged with aggression, I wasn't the only one struggling with ambivalence and guilt. How could *he* allow it? But he did. And I did. And we both walked that fine line between pleasure and danger.

If the world were a different place, a happy rainbow place filled with total peace and harmony, maybe then I *would* come all the time from thinking about making love in a field of daisies. In a perfect, pink-bubble world, I probably wouldn't want to be on the bottom or the top. Then again, pink isn't really my color.

8

Monsters under the Bed

IT WAS SO DISGUSTING, people barfed. Others fainted, and we heard lots of people in the audience definitely walked out. It was gross, violent, superperverted and we couldn't get enough of the details over lunch in our high school cafeteria. It was *Caligula,* the hard-core porn film based on the life of the eponymous Roman emperor.

Produced by *Penthouse* publisher Bob Guccione in 1979, *Caligula* earned a mainstream theatrical release because of its superstars: Malcolm McDowell, Peter O'Toole, Helen Mirren and John Gielgud. Of course, I couldn't care less about them. I was obsessed with the same sick sex scenes that everyone at school was obsessed with, although none of us had actually seen the movie. For weeks, lurid second-, third- and fourth-hand tales filled the halls:

"Okay, so Caligula makes a fist and sticks it in this bucket of Crisco or something and shoves his whole hand up this guy's . . . [*whispered*] butt!"

"Then they tie off this guy's dick with like a rope so he can't pee and then they pour wine down his throat until he's going to explode and then they slice his guts open!"

"A naked woman is riding this bicycle thing that has human tongues attached to the front wheel and when she pedals she gets licked!"

Each new description was greeted with a collective shout of "SICK!" and we thrived on repeating them to the uninitiated. The *Caligula* reports inevitably led to discussions of the grossest sex stories we'd ever heard:

"I know this girl who knew a girl who took Spanish fly and it made her so horny she started *fucking* the stickshift of her boyfriend's VW and when he came back to the car she was dead!"

"Oh, man, that is SICK!"

"No way is that story true."

"It is so! My mom's friend works in the emergency room at Northwest Hospital and she was there the night the dead girl came in."

I suppose I can chalk up my fondness for urban sex legends to an overactive teenage imagination and a lack of sexual experience, but my interest in monstrous tales of sexual depravity didn't fade with the end of adolescence. In my early anti-porn days, I was captivated by chilling rumors of a new sexual horror: snuff films. They were, allegedly, hard-core pornographic films that ended with a woman getting "snuffed out" or murdered. I'd never seen one and didn't know anyone who had, but their existence was incontestable. Snuff films were the gruesome pile at the bottom of that slippery slope, the evil to which all pornography eventually led and the final reason why pornography needed to be stamped out. Unlike my hee-haw responses to *Caligula,* I didn't laugh or joke about snuff films. I listened quietly to the details — young women drugged, gagged, sexually tortured — and repeated them fearfully and with utter seriousness to anyone who would listen. These films were no Hollywood fiction, they were real and deadly.

It's amazing how frequently "What about snuff films?" comes up when I talk about pornography. It's the question that will not die. I want to roll my eyes when I hear it, but I'm careful not to scorn anyone for asking because I've spent considerable time trying to answer the question myself.

In 1989, I read a book titled *Hard Core* by Linda Williams, a film studies professor at University of California, Irvine. It is an academic examination of pornography as a moving, cinematic genre rather than a social nemesis, and her "reading" of the subject was quite refreshing. But to me, the most fascinating section was a brief exposé of a film released in 1976 titled *Snuff.* Until then, I had only heard of snuff the genre, not *Snuff* the movie. Suddenly I felt my fear mutate into that particular combination of anger and confusion that goes hand-in-hand with the realization you've been duped.

Next I rented *Snuff* at my local indie video store, picking it out from an alphabetically disorganized pile of horror movies and Hong Kong action flicks. For the record, *Snuff* is not a porn film. It's a low-budget slasher film about a cult leader named Satán, whose biker-babe followers take drugs and commit crimes for the hell of it. Basically, it's the Charles Manson story right down to the murder of a pregnant starlet, except it takes place in Argentina. There's no sex and only a bit of gratuitous nudity. But tacked on to the end of this insufferable disaster (both technical and directorial) is an obviously fake dismemberment scene that is totally unrelated to the rest of the movie. After the stabbing of the Sharon Tate lookalike, the camera pulls back to reveal the director and the camera crew. The director grabs a female production assistant, makes a few sexual advances toward her, then quickly proceeds to hack her to pieces. The blood spurts, the entrails fly and the whole thing is as believable as Santa Claus.

According to a 1993 article by Eithne Johnson and Eric Schaefer published in the *Journal of Film and Video*, rumors of snuff films existed long before the release of the movie *Snuff*, enough to warrant both New York City Police Department and FBI investigations into the matter. Both came up empty-handed. Rather than dispelling the rumors, though, newspaper reports of the investigations fueled the hysteria with headlines like "'Snuff' Porn — The Actress Is Actually Murdered." Even one of the detectives was quoted as saying, "I am convinced that these films actually exist and that a person is actually murdered," despite his own failure to find any. Ironically, the very lack of hard evidence seemed to further convince people that somewhere, snuff films were being made and consumed in mass quantity. (After all, it's impossible to prove something doesn't exist.) Then a few months later, *Snuff* was released. Even though *Snuff* was revealed to be a hoax, and no covert snuff films were ever found, the anxiety continued to escalate. What if *Snuff* encourages the making of real snuff films? And what about all those people flocking to the theaters, secretly wishing they *could* see a real murder? What a bunch of sickos!

Nobody talks about *Snuff* the movie these days. The tempest it generated has been forgotten. The assumption seems to be that everybody — especially feminists — knows what went down. Yet for the generations who came of age post-*Snuff*, and who feel the subject of pornography is important, most of them don't know. This film was a turning point in the feminist debates about pornography and sexuality. It galvanized the anti-porn feminist faction and led to the identification of pornography as the principal cause of women's oppression. The controversy reaffirmed porn's status as dangerous, low culture and supported the belief that bad images *cause* bad behavior, that pornography *causes* men to commit acts of sexual violence. It was a landslide moment in the history of sexual politics when anti-porn groups, both feminist and religious, became obsessed with demonizing pornography — the effects of which we are still confronting today.

While most people ask me about snuff films out of simple curiosity, a few wield the question like a weapon and they're looking for a fight. Go ahead, Little Miss Porn Cheerleader, let's hear you defend snuff films! Look, if someone presented me with a genuine snuff film there'd be nothing to defend. I would be horrified and sickened. But no one ever has and no one ever will because snuff films, as some kind of readily available, black-market commercial enterprise, don't exist. They're an urban myth.

Don't underestimate the power of myth, though. Myths link us together socially; they influence our moral choices, our political choices; they showcase human nature, bright and dark. They give us reason to believe, which is why the myth of snuff films has survived for so long, despite all the evidence to the contrary. We *want* to believe in snuff films because we have a collective need to believe in sexual monsters.

Throughout history, monsters have reflected our cultural anxieties and fears about sex. Jews, blacks, women, homosexuals — they've all played the demon. The monster, the Other, is born out of social crisis, a threat to the status quo. Belief in monsters unites us against a common enemy, reinforces the rules of sexual conduct, and allows us to justify some of our most extreme actions.

Take witches, for example. They fit the profile of a sexual monster to a T. From the fifteenth to the eighteenth century, thousands of European women were tortured and then burned alive for allegedly practicing witchcraft. The fear? Female sexuality. The monstrous allegation was that witches fornicated with the devil, thereby bringing evil into the world. In reality, they were healers, herbalists and midwives who revered the power of nature. And more often than not, a witch was simply whatever poor soul the mob chose to persecute. Witches gave everyone, Catholic and Protestant alike, a scapegoat for the evils of the day — poverty, disease, violence, mental illness, sexual desire, bad crops, bad luck. Plus, the threat of being marked as a witch kept everyone in line. Even the slightest display of nonconformity, sexual or otherwise, could mean a trip to the fire. Ultimately, the monster justified the massacre.

In much the same way, snuff films meet the requirements of a sexual monster. A belief in snuff films goes hand in hand with the belief that pornography is evil, and that the sexual impulse itself is basically evil and needs to be controlled. Snuff films are a constant reminder of just how bad things can get if left unchecked: women getting fucked up and chopped up, men degenerating into sperm-spurting killing machines. The snuff film panic came at a time when the sexual status quo was being challenged from every cultural corner. Pornography had become chic, even attaining a level of respectability among the middle class. By 1973, the X-rated film *Deep Throat* was playing at theaters around the country, and images of explicit sex were no longer "obscene" in and of themselves; a work now had to be proven to lack serious literary, artistic, political or scientific value. So what new bold strategy could be used to tighten up those loose morals? Linking pornography with murder. Snuff films united two groups who would never have been seen in the same room together — right-wing Christians and radical feminists. The monster gave us a new reason to quash our erotic impulses — snuff or be snuffed — and justified attacks on the First Amendment. By 1985, the Meese Commission recommended greater restrictions of sexually explicit material based on the unconfirmed theory that pornography causes harm. Beginning in the mid-1980s and continuing well into the 1990s, Andrea Dworkin and Catharine MacKinnon proposed anti-porn ordinances in Minneapolis, Indianapolis and Cambridge, Massachusetts, that would allow women to sue for damages for the harm caused by pornography. All three were ultimately voted down, but were a big success at stirring up fear. Censorship continues to be promoted as a necessary defense against the monsters who lurk somewhere out there.

But even for those of us who don't believe in the existence of devils or snuff films, there's no denying a universal fascination with sexual monsters. The success of horrifying movies, the stamina of gross-out urban legends, even the gruesome details of monstrous true crimes printed in the daily paper — they're all testaments to the fact that we're simultaneously attracted and repelled by the forbidden. As much as they frighten us, monsters appeal to us because they reflect our own desires to cross the lines we've drawn, to poke around in the darkest parts of our psyche, to know the Other side of ourselves. At the same time, we don't want to get too close. Monsters hand us a convenient yardstick to measure the distance between Us and Them (which is often frighteningly small) so we can feel secure, "normal" and even superior about our own sexual tastes — I'm not a monster, you are!

I also think sexual monsters and the fear they bring are an antidote to erotic boredom. We scare ourselves on purpose with all sorts of stories because feeling frightened makes us feel alive, utterly conscious of our own existence. Sex will always be exciting as long as there are lines to cross, monsters to confront and questions about just how close we are to the bottom of that slippery slope.

• • •

I was walking through the airport but it felt more like a house of horrors. At every turn, the cover of *Time* magazine leapt out at me. It featured a pasty-faced, bug-eyed toddler ghoulishly lit from below, its mouth hanging open in terror with the headline: "CYBERPORN Exclusive: A new study shows how pervasive and wild it really is. Can we protect our kids — and free speech?" dated July 3, 1995.

The story, which opened with a full-page illustration of a naked androgyne sitting bare-assed on a keyboard and humping a glowing computer monitor, focused on the findings of a study titled "Marketing Pornography on the Information Superhighway." The study, conducted by a team of researchers from Carnegie Mellon University and headed by Martin Rimm, was about to be published in the *Georgetown Law Journal.* What this exhaustive, elaborate, first-time-ever online-porn investigation supposedly proved was that not only is there a lot of porn in cyberspace, but it's getting more and more depraved, catering to users' increasing demands for S/M, bondage, bestiality and pedophilia. The alarmist slant of the article was clear: How will we save the children from this on-screen indecency?

The most often-cited "fact" of the article was this: "In an 18-month study, the team surveyed 917,410 sexually explicit pictures, descriptions, short stories and film clips. On those Usenet newsgroups where digitized images are stored, 83.5% of the pictures were pornographic." It doesn't take a rocket scientist to do the math on that one. Even if it were possible to find, download, view and analyze one image per minute — and it's not — it would take (bringing out my calculator) 637 days nonstop to check out 917,410 of them. Hardly the kind of job you could tackle in eighteen months. Usenet is a decentralized, public network with hundreds of conferences on topics ranging from politics to gardening. I didn't believe that 83.5 percent of it all was pornographic. Neither did a lot of people.

It was war on The WELL, the online service I belong to, and the battle was making national news. In the Media conference, there were soon more than one thousand responses to the topic "Martin Rimm and the Cyberporn Scare" and thousands more in other spin-off discussions. Thanks to a secret, three-way agreement between Marty Rimm, *Time* and the *Georgetown Law Journal,* no outsiders were permitted to read the study and review its conclusions prior to the article's going to press. (After all, everyone knows pornography is bad — who needs proof?)

Mike Godwin, a cyber-rights lawyer for the Electronic

Frontier Foundation (who referred to the entire fiasco as The Rimmjob), along with Donna Hoffman, an associate professor of management at Vanderbilt University, were kicking ass online — discrediting the bogus claims, digging up dirt on Rimm and contending that the "study" was politically biased. The author of the *Time* article, Philip Elmer-Dewitt, was also a WELL member and Godwin was going for his throat:

> Please quote the passage in your story where you *mention* that Rimm, "the study's principal investigator," is an undergraduate EE [electrical engineering] major with no former experience in studying or applying the statistical methodology used in conducting surveys.
> What? You omitted to mention it? Now, why did you do that, Philip?

As it turned out, the nation's most prominent news magazine presented a college kid's unfounded speculations as scientific fact. There was no investigative "team" that had worked long hours conducting a scientific survey. Rimm had acted alone, and his data were hopelessly flawed by his methodology — or lack of one. But his "facts" were now being promoted by U.S. senators and congressmen as another great reason to pass the Communications Decency Act, a federal law aimed to prohibit all "obscene, lewd, lascivious, filthy or indecent" speech on the Internet whether consensual or not; and the general public was freaking out because sex was, once again, dangerously out of control.

Soon, Rimm's credibility began to unravel much closer to home.

The phone rang; it was Susie. "I know Marty Rimm!"

"Did you have cybersex with him?"

"Very funny. He's been E-mailing me for the past few months, presenting himself as my biggest admirer who wanted my expert opinion on erotica for his study of porn on the Internet. I thought it was just some stupid school paper — now it's the cover of *Time* magazine! But the weirdest thing was, he said he was a huge fan of me, Catharine MacKinnon and Camille Paglia. Now how could anyone be a fan of all *three* of us? That'd be like being a Satanist and a Christian at the same time."

"Maybe he secretly wanted to be dominated by all three of you."

"Yeah, well, that wouldn't be his only secret. He even bragged to me about this book he was writing called *The Pornographer's Handbook: How to Exploit Women, Dupe Men and Make Lots of Money.* He promised to send it to me but, golly, it never arrived. Now he claims he was only joking but pieces of it are all over Usenet."

This book, which never materialized except for its brief Usenet appearance, was allegedly aimed at helping adult BBS operators — whose systems Rimm had trolled for porn — choose the most popular photos. It included helpful bits of information like, "For instance, don't always rely on hair color or ejaculate to sell an anal sex image. Remember, above all, that a fat cock in the butt tends to hurt, so make sure the woman always smiles!"

Well, well, well. It appears Marty was grazing both sides of the fence. Godwin linked Rimm to religious right anti-porn groups who assisted in placing and publicizing Rimm's study. Meanwhile, the anti-porn groups were using Rimm to make a case that "cyberporn" was out of control and needed government regulation. Keeping up with the concentric circles of deceit and egomania was mind-boggling, but the monster was easy to spot.

> Monster: Cyberporn
> Fear: Our own uneasiness with sexuality, particularly children's
> Threat: Digital revolution, a huge cultural, economic and social shake-up
> Unity: Republicans and Democrats. What bipartisan do-goodery!
> Action: The Communications Decency Act

Eventually *Time* printed a one-page quasi-retraction, admitting that "serious questions have been raised regarding the study's methodology." Rimm's study was debunked, the numbers were wrong. Eighty-three point five percent of Usenet — or the Internet — is not pornography. In the end, the CDA failed too, declared unconstitutional by the Supreme Court of the United States. But these realities are not what people remember. Branded on the public consciousness is this: Things are getting worse. Lots of innocent children are being corrupted by pornography on the Internet. Society is more sexually depraved now than ever and cyberspace is the most depraved place of all.

In truth, children rarely stumble across pornography on the Net. They don't log on to the Discovery Channel online and accidently end up with torrents of smut streaming out of their computers. Kids look for dirty pictures because they're curious. Now, there's always been plenty of pornography for kids to see in the real world — at the corner newsstand, the video store, thrown out in the neighbor's trash, even hidden with their dad's fishing tackle — so why the hysteria over cyberporn? Because in the good old/bad old days, the methods of preventing pornography from soiling "impressionable" minds seemed more secure and understood. A locked drawer offered parents peace of mind. But computer technology has changed all that. You can't lock up the Internet in a drawer.

At the height of the cyberporn panic, my friend Laura Miller wrote in *Wired* magazine: "What's really at stake in the scare over kids and cyberporn isn't the forcible corruption of presexual minds with insidious electronic filth, but the specter of children's sexual curiosity unfettered by parental controls."

Susie had a slightly different opinion. "It's not kids who have a big problem with sex, it's us — the grown-ups!" she told me. "We want to protect ourselves from the uncomfortable task of dealing with sexual reality."

I think sex is the hardest subject to discuss between parent and child. Almost everyone I know feels uncomfortable talking about sex with their parents. Not sex in the biological abstract, but discussing their own personal sexuality. Even Madonna had trouble writhing around onstage and doing "Like a Virgin" in front of her dad. Photographer Robert Mapplethorpe tried to call the Whitney Museum and have them take down certain S/M photos on the day his parents were going to see his show. As I write this book I keep thinking, *What is my mother going to say when she reads this?* My mother who loves me, who birthed me, who joyously greeted my first pubic hair! Why do I have so much anxiety about her knowing my sexual truths? Because she also taught me to be ashamed about sex — to feel bad about kissing boys, to feel bad about going all the way — and no matter how old I get, the idea of being sexually shamed in her eyes still fills me with dread. The noxious idea that sex is dirty has been far more damaging to me than any pornographic picture.

There's always been tremendous nostalgia over sexual morality; a desire to shuck the frightening present and get back to the good old days. It's comforting to believe that in ancient times — or at least between 1934 and 1963 — human beings were more sexually virtuous and that we can return to that state of purity if we just lay down the law. Censorship is the way to stop the slime, to turn back the clock. The problem is that nobody can show me the Good Old Days on a calendar. When were they? The fifth century? The Summer of Love? The time you got a pony for your birthday? The Days are a very select conflation of happy memories with the unhappiness erased. Time has a tricky way of reducing past disillusionment and strife until they're only a tiny speck. Who really wants to go back to, say, the 1950s when blacks had to ride in the back of the bus, when Senator Joe McCarthy destroyed people's lives in his hunt for suspected Communists, when people chose to die rather than talk about their depression, come out of the closet, deal with their alcoholism or any number of sensitive issues because those realities just didn't fit into the precious picture of the All-American family? I know I don't.

But even if we could time-travel back to the 1950s and peel back the bulletproof layers of repression, we'd find all kinds of sexual interests underneath. (J. Edgar Hoover, now there's a man for all seasons.) Once upon a time we blamed the devil and liquor for being bad sexual influences, now we blame television and the Internet, but people have always been fascinated with sex — be it spiritual, perverted, conventional or monstrous — and they always will be.

About twelve years ago I was in Amsterdam. The city was plastered with red bumper stickers that read "See it all!" So I went to the red light district and into a sex museum that featured historical pornographic etchings, S/M gear on mannequins and audiovisual presentations about exactly what happens if you visit the hookers who sit in the windows. At the back of the gallery there was a set of swinging doors with a skull and crossbones. It warned patrons that they may be shocked by the displays in the darkened room. Of course, it was the busiest part of the museum. Here were all kinds of photos: people hanging weights from their pierced genitals, getting pissed on, eating shit, women fellating dogs and pigs and getting penetrated by snakes and one woman sticking her fist up a horse's ass. I wasn't sure I'd seen it all but I'd certainly seen enough.

These days you don't have to go to Amsterdam to see kinky sex pictures, just go online. I know I'm not the only one who's surfed the Net looking for the most deviant, disgusting image I could find. Inevitably, I find it and then wish I hadn't seen it. Why do it? Because I can. Privately, easily, inexpensively. Technology has freed us from some of the guilt around sex and perhaps it's this idea — of sex with less guilt — that people find so frightening.

I don't believe that the world is now a more vicious or frightening place than it ever was. The Middle Ages were no picnic — disease, superstition, inquisitions, slavery, instruments of torture like the iron maiden and oh, the tooth decay. But I do believe that the monstrous side of human nature is more visible, thanks in no small part to telecommunications technology. With unprecedented speed we hear about the cruelty people inflict upon each other, we see it in living color brought to us via satellite 24 hours a day.

True, there are more — and more explicit — sexual representations in popular culture now than ever before. There are queers kissing during prime time, Howard Stern talking about his small penis on the radio, women crawling around in their underwear on MTV, even the *New Yorker* ran an essay about the joys of getting spanked. It makes lots of people shake their heads and say, "Too much sex! Things are getting worse." The logic goes like this: If sex is bad and there's more sex now than ever before, then things *must* be getting worse. Well, are they? Has all of our exposure to sexual images made us less moral?

When I ask myself if I've been desensitized by the excess of sexual imagery that surrounds me, the truthful answer is yes. Looking at pornography has desensitized me — to pornography. I am rarely as turned on — or off — as I was when I first started looking at it. Much of the magic has disappeared, the way magic does when the pleasure becomes routine. I have become desensitized to the *image* of sex, whether it's a Calvin Klein underwear ad, a Mapplethorpe or a hard-core porn GIF. But I haven't become desensitized to the actual *experience* of sex itself. Not one bit. On the contrary, my critical examination of sex has *sensitized* me to the fragile complexities of real-life, in-the-flesh sexual encounters. My perception of sexual situations and feelings is more acute. I've learned to be more tolerant when it comes to other people's sexual choices, even when it's easier to stay on my high horse. I feel greater empathy toward anyone who mistakes a powerful sexual connection for love and suffers because of it. And through it all, I've gained tremendous faith in my own personal erotic boundaries because I've slammed into them so many, many times.

9

Man-Size

IN THE SUMMER OF 1994, I was back in the studio producing *Cyborgasm 2*, only this time the studio wasn't a glorified closet at Ron Gompertz's house. We were recording at Hyde Street Studios, an expense paid for by our advance from Time Warner. Ron and I had just signed a licensing agreement with the media giant's brand-new AudioBooks division, and visions of gold records were dancing in our heads.

Cyborgasm had been a huge success both commercially and critically. We'd received tons of fan mail from women and men detailing their favorite listening positions ("I stood on the bed and held on to the ceiling pipes with both hands . . ."), their favorite tracks ("Pink Sweatboxes!" "Dirty Fare!" "Circus Whore!") and elaborate suggestions for the next CD ("Okay, it starts with somebody sucking on an ice cube . . ."). One woman wrote, in a perfectly crafted yet shaky script that showed her age, "I never had an orgasm before I listened to this." Most of all, people described how comfortable they felt sharing it with their lovers precisely because there were no pictures, and how exciting it was to engage with the ultimate Virtual Reality tool — their imagination.

I was inundated with calls and demo tapes from women who wanted to contribute to the second CD. It was a sign of the times. Doing phone sex, being a stripper or a dominatrix had acquired the cachet of cool and smart business. I couldn't pick up a magazine without reading about how women were producing, writing or otherwise investigating pornography. In the world of rock, unprecedented numbers of female artists were going public with the power and pleasure of sexual desire. Wholesome-looking Liz Phair softly sang, "I want to be your blowjob queen." Courtney Love, in her babydoll dress and crooked lipstick, screamed "Suck my clit!" during Hole performances before stage-diving into a sea of fans. PJ Harvey, Veruca Salt, Tori Amos — their music dealt with the troubling contradictions and complexities of lust. Do Me Feminists, Riot Grrrls, Angry Chick Rockers — they were everywhere. Maybe the labels were stupid, but what they represented, collectively, was extremely significant: Women's erotic awareness had reached critical mass.

Women would come into the studio and let it rip. During level checks they'd whisper the filthiest stuff in the ear of the Head, our 3-D microphone. My friend Carol Queen walked through the studio door, took off her clothes, dumped a big bag of sex toys on the floor and went to work. Another told a romantic story about strapping it on and fucking her boyfriend in the ass. Some pieces were arty, some cheesy, but almost all of them were, in a word, hot.

Men, on the other hand, were strangely silent. Only a handful, maybe four, had contacted me about contributing. Three were interested in composing music and one forgot to leave his phone number. So I went on a mission to procure sexually explicit stories from men. I aimed high — Anthony Kiedis, Leonard Cohen, Mark Eitzel, Henry Rollins — but I never got past their publicists. Other times, I simply stuck my head out of the studio door and asked any dude who happened to be roaming the halls, "Wanna be on a sex record?" I followed up every lead. I cold-called every friend of a friend who I heard might be interested, and over the course of several months I tracked down and auditioned at least twenty men. They were actors, writers, waiters, white-collar professionals, computer geeks, and all very enthusiastic about revealing their sexual imaginations on tape. I was interested in hearing any and all kinds of fantasies, but was particularly determined to find a hard-core, blow-by-blow, boy-seduces-girl story.

When the guys came to the studio, which was set up like a comfortable bedroom — low light, a few chairs, a futon on the floor, liquor on request — I often gave this direction: "Imagine you're in bed with a woman. You really want to see her come so you tell her a story, a dirty story. She's got her fingers on her clit and she is ready to go. What do you say?" Then I'd leave them alone with the Head and monitor their performance through headphones in the control room. And what did I hear? Things like "I was a horny teenage guy! What did I know? I felt like I could stick my dick in a mortadella and be satisfied" or "And then, like, the dog is barking and her dad is, like, walking in the door and I can't get my pants up! The whole thing was a mess because I couldn't even get a hard-on."

Almost every story was about the hilariously unerotic time

sex went awry. One of them, a piece by monologist Josh Korn-bluth, was so funny, nostalgic and bittersweet that it made the final cut. There were also a few tales of tragically fucked-up love, and a couple of sensual, oh-the-heaven-in-your-eyes de-scriptions, which I considered keepers. But I still wanted a hard-core, boy-seduces-girl story that would make me want to come, and I couldn't seem to get it.

I understand how difficult it is to give an erotic performance even if, in your head, you really want to do it. It's harder still to do it on command. But I decided the real reason why these guys were so disinclined to tell a pornographic story was be-cause they were afraid of looking like pigs, of being judged by their sexual fantasies. To break the ice I'd play a snippet of my own piece, "Puppy." My intent was not only to show them the dynamic range of the female erotic mind but to give them permission to say whatever the hell they wanted to. *Watch as I stand before you, unashamed, even though you have just listened to me chase a dildo across the floor like a dog. Now, it's your turn.*

But the results were less than spectacular. I was puzzled. Men are so familiar with pornographic convention, I thought. This should be easy for them.

· · ·

It was during the production of *Cyborgasm 2* that Stephen and I agreed to Start Seeing Other People in Real Life. The last few times we'd been together had been uneven; perfect moments followed by inauspicious silences and misunderstanding. Other incompatibilities were beginning to surface, too, like the fact that Stephen was an eccentric aesthete who didn't believe in furniture. His living room, for example, was now empty except for a beige clock propped up in one corner, the kind you'd see in an airport, and the entire floor was covered in dead roses and leaves. It was hard to picture us living together. And on top of the frustrating lack of physical contact in our long-distance relationship, I was going absolutely nuts from listening to people fuck and suck all day long and spending every night alone. The virtual, once again, created an overwhelming desire for the real thing.

One Friday evening around quitting time while I was waiting for some digital sound files to back up, I walked into the studio lounge. I sat down on the ratty sofa and absently paged through the *SF Weekly,* one of the city's alternative papers. Suddenly — even though I'd seen them a million times before — I was struck by the number of back-page ads for every imaginable sexual service known, literally, to man. There were blond, brunet, thin, fat, busty, flat, young, experienced, innocent, black, white, Asian and Latina schoolgirls, mistresses, naughty nurses and chicks with dicks who were on call twenty-four hours a day to come to his erotic rescue. Not a single one offered me the same professional courtesy.

I moved along to the personals, where everyone is extremely attractive and likes food, movies and talking. There were also tons of ads — almost all of them placed by men — seeking brief sexual liaisons. Under the heading Men Seeking Women were scores of married men looking for younger, discreet women to have a casual affair with, or men wanting to be dominated by women or both. *Wait, here's one: **suCK**. Former Calvin Klein model wants to free your ass.* Model boy's promises included stunning beauty, sexual experience, insatiability and postmodernist theory. I looked around to make sure the coast was clear. I got up, walked to the pay phone, dropped in a quarter before I lost my nerve. I dialed the voice mail box number listed next to the ad. There was no greeting, just a beep. I hung up and redialed. Same thing. I went ahead and left a short message — my first name, phone number, my availability for drinks that evening. "Oh, and possibly more than that," I said in my breathiest, sexiest voice.

When I got home, I mixed myself a vodka martini with two olives and began pacing. About forty-five minutes had passed since I called Calvin. No response. In fact, there were no messages on my machine at all. I dug out my emergency cigarettes and lit one. Bad idea. The combination of alcohol and nicotine always makes me nauseated. I brushed my teeth and examined them in the mirror. I opened and closed the refrigerator. I lay down on the bed and masturbated. I got up, made myself another drink. I flipped through my address book, just in case I'd overlooked any platonic possibilities that could be exploited. Nope. I sat in the dark watching the green numbers on my digital clock change shape and thinking, The Hi-Tech Sex Chick. If they only knew.

•••

A few months later I am introduced to an extraordinarily gorgeous man who seems to like my direct approach to sex. We're having a drink and at one point he says, "I could just kiss you!"

"You could," I say, and he does.

The chemistry is heavy. We start making out at the table.

"Want to see my etchings?" I inquire.

"Thought you'd never ask." We go back to my place and do it. Superb relief at last.

The next morning, I wake up greedy. I kiss him and rub up against him, take little bites of him. He is rather unresponsive. Finally there is nothing left to do but come right out with it: "I am so horny!" I let out a small, exasperated squeak and flop back on the bed. He just laughs.

"Stay horny until tonight," he says enthusiastically. "Sex in the morning, it's a personal thing."

Is it my breath? My face in the morning sun? What? "Okay," I say, trying not to let my huge disappointment show.

When tonight rolls around we're at a restaurant and there's not a lot to say. Not that there has to be. Not like our conversation the night before was deeply philosophical or anything. I begin to feel incredibly self-conscious and unpretty. I look at my cuticles and wonder if I should have done my nails. I feel ugly in my clothes. Everything is wrong. But then he reaches over and takes my hand. "Let's go back to my house," he says.

Once inside his apartment, he puts on Steely Dan, loud. He sits down in an armchair, does a few bong hits and starts flipping through a magazine. I sit on the couch, speechless. *Why aren't his hands all over my excruciatingly aroused body? I've waited all day.* "So, what do you wanna do?" he asks. I walk over and straddle the chair, take his face in my hands and whisper the absolute truth. "I want to fuck you and I wish you felt the same way." He shakes his head. No.

Uh-oh. Maybe I shouldn't have used the word *fuck*. Maybe I should have said something more sensitive and dreamy, like, I want to feel you inside me.

"Why not?" I ask.

He squirms, but eventually the truth comes out. He really likes me blahblahblah and he enjoys my company blahblahblah but the reason he didn't want to have sex in the morning was because he was beginning to think it might not have been a good idea to sleep together in the first place.

"Is this the 'Let's Just Be Friends' talk?" He stares at me. I give him my views on erotic friendship and how I don't want to marry him or have his baby — even though, god, what a beautiful baby it would be! — I just want a bit of intrigue, a warm body. I just want sex.

"Look, I've been with women who say all they want is sex but they really want more. Like a relationship. And it's just a big headache to me." He reaches for a bag of Drum and rolls himself a cigarette.

I decide to do the only respectable thing: get up and go home. I'm not going to beg for sex. Am I? When I start to put on my coat he says he wants me to stay. He kisses me as he unbuckles his jeans and puts my hand on his hard cock. We go to bed. He comes, I don't, and he doesn't seem to notice. The next morning I leave feeling unsatisfied and angry, and my eyes hurt from sleeping in my contact lenses.

I go for a long walk in Golden Gate Park and cross-examine myself.

He thinks I want a relationship? What bullshit!

Oh, really? If all you wanted was sex, then why did you have to see him the very next day?

Because the sex was great and I wanted more. Is that so wrong?

Maybe he wasn't as impressed. Or maybe for him, once was enough. Is that so wrong?

So he was in it for the conquest. This relationship crap is a smoke screen, a convenient veil for an uglier truth: I fucked you and now the game is over, mission accomplished, so get a clue.

But I had to admit I was in it for many of the same reasons. I wanted to boost my ego, reassure myself of my sexual desirability. I wanted to come — and go. Or at least that's what I kept telling myself. Now I was wishing that he'd asked me to spend the day with him. It was crazy. What happened to my one-track mind? My big plans for emotional detachment?

And what happened to the idea that all men want is sex, all the time? All my life I'd operated under the illusion that men are largely indiscriminate and would, well, stick their dick in a mortadella if they had to. Since it's traditionally fallen to women to say no, I'd always thought I just had to say yes to sex and men would fall at my feet — even though my own experience often proved me wrong. Remember poor old James V., my teenage boyfriend who almost got his neck broken by my father? I practically begged him to fuck me, too, and he refused. Over the next fifteen years quite a few men turned me down, but I still found myself believing the hype: Men are sluts. What a sucker!

At least I'm not the only sucker. Plenty of women I know have been left bewildered and frustrated by men who say no to sex. It's a phenomenon that seems to happen quite frequently these days. My friend Bill thinks it's cosmic payback. "The universe wishes to maintain its balance," he wrote in an E-mail. "When women acquire male-power (money, independence, freedom of choice), men acquire female-power (they become cunt-teasers). What did you expect?"

• • •

Two weeks later I was in a hotel on the Las Vegas strip. Susie Bright insisted that I make the arrangements since it was my idea. I picked up the phone and dialed.

"My friend, uh, Sue and I would like to hire two male escorts," I said in my bravest voice. From the zillions of choices in the Yellow Pages I randomly picked Priority Male, advertising Adult Male Entertainers, 24 Hours, All Major Credit Cards Accepted.

The man who answered the phone was very nice. He told me the "entertainers" would be $125 apiece and that they would come to our hotel room for one hour, do a striptease and get completely naked.

"Suppose we wanted *more* than that," I said, trying to be discreet yet direct, "like an erotic massage or perhaps even *more* than that?"

"That would be something to negotiate with the entertainers," he replied. I thanked him and hung up.

"I'm not paying for some guy to come up here and just take his clothes off," Susie said. She was doing porn star poses on our California king bed at the Imperial Palace and giggling at her reflection in the mirror on the ceiling. "We need to make a list, a completely self-centered wish list, of all the things we want and then place our order."

"You're a genius." I grabbed a pencil and paper and started writing.

"Two bisexual guys," she said.

"No mustaches or hairy backs."

"Must be at least five foot ten."

"Preferably with dark long hair."

"Cock size?" Huge, of course.

"Black, white, Hispanic okay."

"Sense of humor and literacy a plus."

I called the agency back and laid it on the line. We wanted the boys to put on a little sex show and then pleasure us. The agency promised us two of the hottest babes, satisfaction guaranteed. I penciled in our *entertainment* for eight o'clock that evening.

I chose Las Vegas because I knew it was a hotbed of prostitution. Of course, some of my friends couldn't understand why I would want to hire a prostitute. If I wasn't too picky, couldn't I walk into any bar and get picked up? Too much work. Others righteously announced that anybody who would pay for sex is a loser. Who were they kidding? We all pay for sex. Some of us just don't use cash.

As men have known for thousands of years, there are plenty of benefits to paying for sex, like no messy relationship problems. Ladies, you don't need to wonder, Will he call me tomorrow? You don't need to worry about whether he really likes you or is being truthful when he says your body is gorgeous, because it's his JOB to make you feel like the most special thing in the world. In fact, you don't have to lift a finger. How is his erection doing? Is he having a good time? Did he come? Who cares! The only thing that matters is your satisfaction. This doesn't mean you should act like a snot-nosed prima donna, but it's very important not to lose sight of who's servicing whom. In theory, anyway.

Around 7:00 P.M., I decided we needed mood lighting. I left our room and ran up and down the entire Strip for nearly an hour looking for candles. Meanwhile Susie was in a total panic, worried that she'd have to handle the *entertainment* all by herself. Upon my return, I tore off all my clothes, put on fresh lipstick and climbed in the Olympic-size tub, conveniently located right next to the bed, and poured in the bubble bath. I mentally checked the list: candlelight, cocktails from room service, condoms, Susie in some skimpy black lingerie, me under the bubbles. The presentation was very Dean Martin.

By 8:15, our dates still hadn't shown up. To distract us from our nervousness, I asked Susie about her highest expectations for the evening.

"I want smooth operators. I want them to work at making us feel relaxed and beautiful, and be concerned with our sexual pleasure, too," she said. "You?"

"I want them to be good-looking, otherwise I'm sending them back."

"How're you gonna do *that?*"

I thought for a moment about exactly how I *would* do that. "I'll say, 'Thanks very much for coming here tonight but I don't think it's going to work out. You're not quite what we had in mind.' Then I'll call the agency and tell them to send someone else — pronto! Guys do that all the time when they order hooker room service."

Just then there was a knock on the door. Enter Michael, a blond, and Riks, a brunet. To be honest, they were both a little too buff for my taste, had a little too much gel in their new-wave hairdos and just barely made the height requirement. But Michael, twenty-four, had a very lovely face and perhaps Riks, twenty-seven, had something to offer that I hadn't seen yet. (I couldn't decide if Riks had a European accent or a speech impediment. I think his name was actually "Rex.")

It turns out that being naked in the bathtub was an excellent idea because it immediately quelled any suspicions that I was a cop. (Officers cannot be nude when they make a vice bust.) It also sped up the service. Soon we were all standing on the bed, frottaging, with Susie and I taking turns being sandwiched in the middle. I asked what usually happens when women hire entertainment.

"Mostly it's for bachelorette parties," Michael said. "We strip, the girls get drunk and watch, act wild. And if anything else happens, it's usually them wanting to do stuff to us."

"Like what?"

"Like . . ." Michael lowered his voice. "Like they want to give us blow jobs and act all slutty in front of us. It's kind of the opposite of what you'd expect."

Michael's boyish innocence was a real turn-on. So was his incredible endowment. Riks, however, was really starting to bug me, especially when he suggested I get down on my knees and do a little cock worship. *Funny you should ask, because under different circumstances . . .* "I don't think so," I said. Instead, I suggested that he and Michael worship each other. Michael made a big face and confessed that he was straight. A show was out of the question despite the fact that we had specifically requested it. "All right then," I said, switching gears, "how about both of you worship me?" Michael responded immediately but Riks wouldn't budge. He didn't go down on girls.

So I ignored him. Occasionally I'd look in the mirror on the ceiling and find Riks looking at himself, stroking his big ego. I wanted Susie to join *our* pile, but she was talking to Riks and skillfully applying her hands and mouth.

Suddenly I found myself getting bored and wondering, Has it been an hour yet? I changed my mind. I didn't want to fuck this man, this stranger. Even with a condom, it felt too risky. Not physically, but emotionally. I was feeling good about the whole encounter and I didn't want the very intimate act of sexual intercourse to mess things up. Maybe it would be great but maybe it would suck. It might leave me feeling empowered or I might feel like shit. Only one thing was certain: I'd never fucked a man and felt absolutely nothing afterward.

And despite all my hot air over being serviced, I never really expected to come. I knew I'd be too distracted by the newness of the experience and wouldn't be able to focus. But just as I was thinking about getting dressed I felt this tiny tingle — the sensation of genuinely becoming aroused. I let myself go until I had, not an orgasm exactly, but sort of an orgasmic wave. It felt very good and I made a lot of noise to signal The End.

As the boys were getting dressed, Michael's beeper went off and he asked if he could make a quick call. His phone voice was sweet and muffled, mixed with a sense of urgency. He hung up.

"That was my girlfriend calling to tell me not to forget to pick up diapers on the way home. For our baby." He smiled. I smiled back and pushed a twenty-five-dollar tip into his hand as he walked out the door.

Afterward, Susie and I talked about the events of the evening. I was surprised by my sense of satisfaction and Susie's sense of obligation. She had felt responsible for Riks's sexual happiness and was now bumming out.

"I guess I'm better at being the whore."

"Oh sweetie, that's not true. We just need better whores. Next time we're going to Boca Raton," I announced. "I read this book about gigolos that said the working men down there are real charmers. They speak several languages and even know which fork to use. They cost more, but we're worth it."

Well, we never went to Boca Raton. The experience in Vegas had been enough. It wasn't disappointing, but it wasn't particularly fulfilling, either. I still wanted intrigue and a warm body next to mine and exquisite sex. But I wanted so much more than that.

•••

A week or so after my Las Vegas adventure, I telephoned my friend Laura Miller for some girl talk. Out of habit, I started slipping back into my why-I-can't-get-laid routine and she sternly corrected me.

"Lisa, you *can* get laid. It's just that you don't want to have sex with the men who want to have sex with you. Do you think B——— or M——— would turn you down?"

"No."

"See? You're looking for a certain kind of quality erotic experience with someone you're sexually attracted to, who's attracted to you and shares your interests and desires. You need someone like, I don't know, the Marlboro Man."

"A macho cowboy is the last thing I need."

"I'm talking about a man so secure in his masculinity that he's not going to be intimidated by who you are, how much sex you want, what you write about for a living or your emotional longings. The Marlboro Man. Trust me."

10

The Fall

"**F**ALLING IN LOVE IS like stepping in dog shit."

"What?" My voice dropped to a suspicious whisper. "That's blasphemy. What about all the great poets like William Blake and . . . and Leonard Cohen? Without the cruel beauty of love and romance they'd be nowhere."

Betty Dodson laughed and ran a hand through her short silver hair. Her big and perfect white teeth caught the glow from the cheap lamp on the cocktail table. God, she looked great for sixty-five.

She downed the rest of her drink and I raised my glass in a deficient little motion of cheers, then swallowed. *I don't think I've ever been this depressed in my entire life.* Stephen and I were officially splitsville. He met someone new.

I was at Mistress Kat's Fabulous at 50 Ball, a fiftieth-birthday bash held at San Francisco's Great American Music Hall, given in honor of publisher and S/M educator Kat Sun-love. It was a Who's Who of sex people. Feminist porn director Candida Royalle was there, in a red rubber dress and red stockings. She waved and came closer. "I made my singing debut in this place, a song about a little tomato," she told me as Veronica Vera, who runs Miss Vera's Finishing School for Boys Who Want to Be Girls, a crossdresser academy in New York City, scribbled down her E-mail address on a business card and handed it to me. Splinters of conversation shot past me. Photographer and performance artist Annie Sprinkle, who once did a piece titled Public Cervix Announcement where she invited audience members to look up a speculum and see her os, was talking about her latest Hawaiian tantric sex retreat. Joani Blank, Good Vibrations founder, showed off pictures of her granddaughter.

"Who's the guy in the tuxedo with a bone through his nose?" someone wondered out loud.

"Oh, that's Fakir Musafar."

I mused on how far I'd come: from being totally grossed out by those naked pictures of Fakir hanging on a meat hook to sharing cocktail wienies with him. It was the kind of party I once dreamed about — hobnobbing with the SF sex intelligentsia — and now here I was, feeling lonely in a crowd of cheerful perverts who would no doubt supply me with any sexual party favor I could dream up. It only made me feel worse.

In the hours immediately preceding Kat's party, I had a very lousy conversation with Stephen. He told me he was serious about a woman who lived in New York City and was, therefore, ending our sexual relationship. Though we'd been Seeing Other People for several months, I never expected he might actually kick me out of his bed completely.

"Lisa, we've been making the transition from lovers to friends for a long time now," he pointed out. In my fairy-tale mind, I imagined we'd always be both.

The last thing I wanted to do was go to a party with *sex people,* but Susie insisted on it. She gave me her it's-good-to-get-out pep talk while she ransacked her closet for an outfit for herself, and I lay facedown on her bed, yelling into the pillows. "Every time I think about Stephen and his new girlfriend, it feels like my head is going to explode. Or I'm going to throw up. I need a lobotomy."

"No. You need exactly the opposite," she said, over the sound of metal clothes hangers being raked across a bar. "You need to have lots of masochistic fantasies about the kind of sex they have together. Imagine the most pornographic thing you can. Picture the new girl with her freshly spanked ass up in the air, takin' it really hard from behind while he shoves a —"

"STOP!"

"Look, the fastest way for you to burn out your jealousy is to imagine the worst. Think the unthinkable. Leave no stone unturned. Once you can handle that, you're over it." She sighed. "What the hell am I going to wear? Everyone expects me to come dressed as a giant piece of cleavage."

"Try to look like Gladys Kravitz from *Bewitched.*" I rolled over. "Pajamas, curlers in your hair, some green facial gunk. That'll turn some heads."

Susie decided on pink flannel pajamas with Barbie dolls on them. I wore a simple black dress to match my spirit. I considered accessorizing it with one of those stickers that says, "Hello, I'm . . ." and filling it in with, "a sex-negative feminist. GO AWAY."

At the party, I'd plopped down next to Betty because I wanted her to remind me, as she had in the past, that falling in love was a trap, a lie, a temporary ego collapse! and I should forget about it before it destroyed me.

I first met Betty Dodson when I was working at *On Our Backs* and I took her Bodysex Workshop, which she'd been hosting since 1973. It was a two-day class held in the nude that gave women a chance to talk about their bodies, fantasies, orgasms — or lack of them — and yes, to teach women how to masturbate with a little help from the Hitachi Magic Wand. Betty was funny, foulmouthed and a testament to the wisdom that comes with age, so I decided to interview her for the magazine. Of all her insights into sexuality and relationships, though, it was her comments on romantic love that made me feel as if I'd just been slapped. "I swore off romance in 1969, a few years after my divorce," she told me then. "When people fall in love they 'become one.' The problem is, which one? I didn't want to bend to somebody else's will. Fuck that. Falling in love is like taking a hostage. We want to nail them down and . . . we want vows of monogamy and then we want to get married. In that whole process, believe me, romance goes down the tube." I'd listened to plenty of people — I was one of them — deride marriage as just another institution to get locked up in, but I'd never heard anyone be so critical about the falling-in-love part.

Now here I was, four years later, coming back for a dose of the same medicine. I heard Betty's glass go *clink* on the table and saw her mouth moving. I snapped back to attention.

"As you get older it's hard not to be set in your ways," Betty continued, "and you're right that I'm hard on romantic love and hard on marriage — although I'm trying to be less militant — because those are the two things that fuck women up the most. I've been a teacher for over twenty-five years and I've listened to the tragedy that these two things have brought into women's lives. They strip us of our power, of our creativity, of our personhood. Romantic love that drifts into a marriage is devastating for women. It's the cancer of our sexuality." She paused. "The truth for me is that there's nothing more exciting than power. I don't mean power over other people but the power over my own life."

The next morning I woke up at six because some nut with a gun was running down the middle of Valencia Street firing off rounds and screaming, "Now you've really pissed me off, you pussy-whipped chump bastards!" Blam. Blam. Then everything went quiet. Now wide awake, I wondered why my head was pounding. Oh yeah, the party last night. Drowning my sorrows. Stephen.

A freak emotional storm rolled in, like *that*. I burst out crying and watched a rerun of Stephen taking the blindfold from my eyes.

"How do you feel?"

"Transformed, enlightened, ecstatic."

"Ah, the markings of a saint." He laughed, kissed me.

Now we're in the men's room at Grand Central Station. It's empty. I'm straddling one of the cold white sinks. My pants dangling around one ankle. "What if someone walks in?" I ask.

"Then they can watch."

I hear his quiet English voice, mouth so close to my ear, and the words run together: press up against me, pretty, dirty, sweetheart, love. Does he tell her the same things?

I got out of bed and stood naked in front of the full-length mirror. It was the first time I actually saw the sand running out of my hourglass figure. I lifted my right arm. *Look, the beginning of underarm flab.* I jiggled the skin with my left hand as proof. *And my eyes.* I moved in for a close-up. *Swollen — ruined for the day from this!* My breasts looked less pert, more pendulous — pendulous being the nice way of saying "sagging" — than I ever remembered and there would only be more sag, not less, to come. *Old. I'm getting old.* It wasn't just my youthful appearance I saw slipping away, but my fertility. I had a finite number of years left before my baby-making days were over. How many more chunks of time would I invest in fleeting relationships before all my time was used up? Tick, tick.

At least I don't have to go to the office looking like this, I thought, because I'm already there.

I was living alone in a small overheated apartment on a busy street in the heart of the Mission District, a real multi-culti mix of Latino families, dykes and slackers, and had just started spending every day at home, alone, working on this very book. I assumed my new writerly life would be sanguine, even peaceful. I hadn't counted on the jackhammers tearing up the sidewalk, delivery trucks and buses off-gassing right underneath my window, the nonstop eight-octave car alarm medleys, blasts of mariachi music, the bliss-ninny drum circle held in the New Age bookstore right below me and people screaming bloody murder from nine to five. Whoever said insanity is an occupational hazard for writers was right.

It was April 1995. The first spring I ever resented. The longer days, the happy blossoms, the perfume of life in the air — I hated the whole conspiracy. I watched my social life drop like a penny down an elevator shaft, now that I was living like a mole in my secret world of work and suffering. I craved human contact but continually pushed it away. When I was in, I wanted out. When I was out, all I wanted to do was go home. Being in the presence of other people was exhausting. I had nothing to add to the conversation except for the boring, broken-record details of my own misery. I wanted to be alone with my loneliness, to examine it in private and marvel over its crushing weight.

Romance? I was ambivalent. I adored it, I despised it. I yearned for it, yet felt so betrayed and humiliated by it. With the same intensity that it had once inspired me, it now devastated me, shattering my confidence not just in relationships but in life itself.

My friends didn't understand why I was so full of despair. "I thought it wasn't really working out with this guy anyway," they'd say. And they were right. It was the familiarity of how, in the end, it just never works out that was killing me.

I grew suspicious of the telephone. It rarely rang anymore, and when it did, it was usually Stephen calling to tell me two things: he's sorry and he loves me. I pretended I couldn't decide whether to pick up or not when I heard his voice on the answering machine. What a tiresome little drill. I always picked up. Because I desperately wanted to communicate with him. I loved him, and in my heart of hearts I wanted to accept and respect our changing relationship. But all of my sexual feelings for him were still intact. I didn't know what to do with them, where to put them, how to turn them off, which is what I would have to do for us to just "be friends." So I sabotaged myself at every turn. Conversations started out in good faith but often ended with me hissing, Don't call me again. Which, of course, was only a sick test to see if he cared enough to call me again.

Occasionally, there were other callers.

"Hey, Lisa, you there? It's Ron." I picked up. "Looks like our big record deal is going belly up," he said. "At first I thought the reason everyone at Time Warner stopped returning my calls was because they hated me, but it turns out they were all too busy getting fired." The AudioBooks division was being reorganized, and *Cyborgasm* was getting bounced around like a hot potato.

"So where are we now?"

"In the children's division. I just got a letter written on Time Warner Kids stationery. Swear to god."

"Well they're not going to release an X-rated CD on a kiddie label — nobody's that stupid. Are they?"

"What this really means is that plans for *Cyborgasm 3* are dead and the other two records are out of print until we hire a lawyer and buy back the rights."

Ron and I talked for a while, grieving over the death of our gold record.

"Remember when we were the darlings? When they wined and dined us, told us how much they loved us?" He laughed.

"The honeymoon always ends, doesn't it?"

Once upon a time I believed experience and wisdom would teach me how to spin romantic insanity into a rational act. If only I could use my head and get smart about this love stuff. If only I could stop being so expectant, expended, paranoid and sentimental and learn to play it cool — oh, the free time I'd have. But falling in and out of love is not something I learned how to do; it's not a logical process. I've always felt as if I was dragged into this crazy-making, vulnerable behavior against my will. I never made a conscious choice to fall in love, it was effortless; gravity sucked me down. I never stood up and decided to fall out, either. And try as I might to restrain myself when I didn't get what I wanted, it proved nearly impossible to do. A rather maddening reality for someone who considers herself in control.

I was out of my mind with jealousy over Stephen's new relationship, which was — how convenient! — unfolding in cyberspace. Spending every day in front of my computer writing made it so easy, under the pretense of work, to log on to The WELL and check my E-mail and then quickly telnet over to ECHO and follow their burgeoning affair. To the uninitiated their posts were innocuous — but not to me. I knew where they went, what they did, how often they each logged on, when they were YO'ing each other, and read between the lines of every special wink and coo meant just for each other. I was shocked by my jealousy. I absolutely disapproved of jealousy! How could I be behaving this way? What was next? CYBERSEX QUEEN HACKS EX-LOVER TO BITS! on the front page of the *New York Post?*

Finally I dialed ECHO proprietor Stacy Horn, explained the situation and then begged her to close my free account. "Oh, Stacy, please, you've got to shut me down because I can't stop torturing myself!" I'm sure I wasn't the first person to demand an intervention, because Stacy knew exactly what to do. "I'm going to change your password so you can't access your account," she said, "but I won't close it. Someday, probably sooner than you think, you'll be in a different place and ready to come back."

Onward, onward. I dragged myself out of the house and into a record store, searching for the usual: hope, solace, an explanation. I was browsing through the Es, wishing that Brian Eno had made a record called "Music for Depression," when the polyester-pants-wearing hipster behind the counter cranked up "Love Will Keep Us Together," the Captain and Tenille's breezy '70s pop hit. *You! You belong to me now/Ain't gonna set you free now!* What a sick little codependent drama posing as a love song. I felt trapped in a bad romantic comedy. Out on the street carefree, billboard-size couples laughed and laughed and puffed on their Newports. The television in the Laundromat asked me, "Are you wondering if you'll ever find that perfect someone?" *Christ, how did they know?* "Then pick up the phone and call the Psychic Yahoo Network now!" I couldn't stand in a supermarket checkout line without being hustled by magazines trying to sell me "Ten Ways to Win His Heart!" or "How to Fall in Love and Stay There Forever!"

There oughtta be a law, I thought. Pundits and policy-makers are always so outraged over images of sex — Look! A bare ass! People fucking! Why don't these moral crusaders devote a little time to stomping out the heavily commercialized, counterfeit ideals of love and romance? Happily Ever After is the carrot everybody's chasing, and it's screwing up people's lives on such a massive scale it's impossible to count the casualties.

All the books and seminars and magic elixirs and love maps that comprise the How to Find True Love industry drive me nuts with their quick and easy-to-follow directions for intimacy. As if finding love is some kind of concrete, step-by-step process that can be readily mastered, just like learning to rebuild your car's engine or speak Chinese. Sure, building your self-esteem or simply getting out of the house increases your chances of making an intimate connection, but the biggest problem with love maps is that *there are no maps*. There's nothing you can do to make someone love you. It either happens or it doesn't. It's the kind of situation you can't control, the kind that leaves you feeling utterly helpless. And helplessness is the worst feeling on the entire emotional spectrum. I'll take guilt, jealousy or anger over it any day.

•••

"Why don't you get out of town for a while?" Susie suggested. "Go someplace nice, treat yourself. Maybe one of those fancy spas where they wake you up with a gong, give you a facial and then send you out on a seventy-mile hike."

A trip. What an excellent idea. I booked a ticket to New York City.

My reasons for going were ironclad: I needed to conduct necessary research for my book. I needed serious retail therapy. I wanted the company of some old friends. The trip had absolutely nothing to do with Stephen. *I'm not even going to tell him I'm coming. And if I happen to run into him on the street, I'll act completely nonchalant. Or maybe I'll phone him while I'm there just to announce that I'm too busy to get together. Maybe I should call him after I get back to tell him how sorry I am that I was in New York for two whole weeks and didn't have time to call.* As I packed my suitcase, I wondered: Would he like me in this dress? These shoes?

I stayed uptown with one of my dearest and oldest friends, Dan. I've known him so long, I remember when he still had hair. I arrived the second weekend of June and we spent it doing classic New York things: cruising around Manhattan on the Circle Line, walking around Bethesda Fountain, checking out the Chagalls in Lincoln Center. He read me a poem by Raymond Carver called "You Don't Know What Love Is (an evening with Charles Bukowski)" while I took a bubble bath, and cracked me up with his observations on toilets around the world.

"Did I tell you about the ones in Japan? You press a button and they blast water right up the crack of your ass. Man, I couldn't tear myself away!"

He also let me cry on his shoulder, literally. "Everything's gonna be okay," he'd say softly, while he stroked my hair. I honestly didn't know if I believed him.

True to my objectives, I went to the library almost every day and read old magazine articles about the history of sexual revolutions. I went to the Museum of Television and Radio and watched episodes of *That Girl* and *Love, American Style* and *Laugh-In*. (Very, very important!) I charged up a storm in SoHo shoe stores. I interviewed friends and colleagues on their sexual opinions and ideas, and in the process couldn't help but ask what they did to get over a bad breakup.

"First I write in my journal, IT IS OVER about a million times," Richard, a photographer, said. "Then I dig out some bad pictures of them and think about how unattractive they really were."

"I read Samuel Beckett," Allison said. "You know, 'I can't go on. I'll go on.'"

"I like to call and hang up," Debbie said. "But now with Caller ID and star-69, that whole strategy has gone to hell."

I found myself walking in front of Stephen's place. Just seeing the building, the doorman in the foyer and the hallway that led to the elevator filled me with an inexplicable sense of hope. It was all proof that Stephen existed, that once upon a time things between us were perfect and good and maybe, if I did the right thing, I could get back to that place. A few days later I sent him an E-mail. "I walked past your house again today. I seem to be finding myself in front of your house when I am in this town. Old habit, I guess."

We ended up meeting in the evening in Tompkins Square Park. The air was warm, it was almost summer. We sat down on a park bench. I looked at him and looked away, down at my hands, the ground, the way my toes looked in my sandals, the disgusting pigeons. *Why did I come here?* A cockroach skittered across my bare thigh. I didn't even flinch. The silence lasted forever, and then I lost it. Some people when they cry look quite lovely: quiet delicate tears running down their cheeks, that look of beatific acceptance. But oh no, not me. I started to slide off the bench as if my spine was melting.

"Lisa, please, c'mon." Stephen pulled me up and we started walking back to his apartment with me clutching his arm and stumbling along like somebody who'd just been pulled from a plane wreck.

We sat on cushions in the middle of his living room floor, which was still covered in those dead roses and leaves, while I sobbed. He didn't know what to say except "I love you" and "I'm sorry." I was mad at him for not saying more. I nearly made the sign of the cross and begged Jesus in Heaven to save me. I couldn't believe that after all of my critical remodeling of God, I still defaulted to Man in a White Beard when the situation got desperate. I wondered if it was possible to choke to death on your own tears. I had to leave. I took a cab back uptown.

The next morning Dan left on a business trip. Perfect. I pulled the shades down in his bedroom and blasted the A/C. I brought in a mop bucket filled with ice and a fifth of Absolut, and set it down by the side of the king-size bed. I made a few choice selections from my traveling stash of sedatives that I'd amassed over the years. Fuck trying to cheer myself up, I thought, as I swigged from the bottle. I'm going down Charles Bukowski–style. You don't know what love is! Fuckers!

I woke up around five. Took a shower. Ordered in some sushi. Tried to watch TV, but the remote was too complicated. Went back to bed and continued down the ladder, wondering just how low I could go. On the third day, I ran out of supplies. And out of pity.

What's with the melodrama, Palac? Are you going to kill your-self? Is that what this is all about? Because if it is, don't do a half-assed job. You want to die, then die. Chop-chop. But don't use your pain to try to make someone love you. The voice of reason paused. *Don't be like your mother.*

The last thought stopped me cold.

And, oddly, it reminded me of a commercial I used to hear on the radio. An overenthusiastic, game show–style announcer said, "Imagine a machine you could put on your head that would teach you foreign languages!" It always cracked me up and got me picturing all sorts of machine-heads. *Imagine a machine that you could put on your head that would teach you how not to be like your parents!* That one, I figured, would be the size of a washing machine.

I never met anyone who wanted to be *more* like their parents. Growing up is all about separating ourselves from them; carving out our own identities, rigging our own failures and victories. Still, I often see my mother's face when I look in the mirror. Not only because of the physical resemblance, but because I find myself doing the same things, saying the same things she does. Sometimes I'm proud of our similarities, sometimes amused and other times, very frightened by them.

My mother bet all of her chips on beauty, married a man she didn't love and lived her whole life believing that suffering is love. I've always been terrified of making those same mistakes — I didn't want to go down that road. And the afternoon I woke up in Dan's bed, fresh out of liquor and excuses, I decided I never would. I couldn't let it happen.

I got up and opened the shades. Stephen, Stephen, I sighed. What to do about him? Us? Twisting the knife was so much work. Besides, what I really wanted more than anything was for both of us to be happy. I loved him, and when you love somebody you're supposed to *act* loving, not helpless, hysterical, passive-aggressive and jealous. *Let him go.*

Leaning my forehead against the window, I saw Stephen rising up into the sky over Broadway like a beautiful star while I waved good-bye like a queen on a parade float. I felt so relieved. I realized I could spend my entire life waiting for life to stop being difficult, trying to outrun loneliness, blaming someone else for failing to serve me my happiness on a silver platter. Or not.

Sitting on the edge of the bed, I grabbed my journal and, after pages and pages of dizzying rage against the universe for doing so many shitty things to me, I wrote:

If I am destined to be single for the rest of my life, then
I am going to crawl out of my hole and make it a great

life. If having friends who love me and work that's interesting is as good as it gets, then it is a life worth living. And if Prince Charming never fathers my child, well, there's always the sperm bank. No one can give me the deliverance I long for except me.

11

All Ball and No Chain

"**E**VERYTHING'S FUCKED!**"** Four days after my Choose Life decision, I was back in California at Susie's Santa Cruz getaway having a huge tantrum because a FedEx package I'd sent had been delayed by the Unabomber crisis. I marched into the living room and was in the middle of my next dazzling sentence when I realized — oh shit — there's company. Jon, Susie's longtime live-in lover, was sprawled out on the floor and a very attractive couple was sitting on the couch, both of them slight, young and Mediterranean-looking. They were dressed similarly in long-sleeve flannel shirts over T-shirts and shorts. I was haglike: glasses, greasy hair, hairy legs, stale coffee breath and suffering a minor zit attack.

Susie introduced me. "Lisa, this is Andrew and Laura." I nodded hello. "We were just thinking about lunch. Wanna join us?"

"Are you going to that New Age place where the food is made out of twigs?" I asked.

"No." Susie's eyes narrowed as she made her I-am-SO-annoyed-with-you face.

"The place where they don't let you use knives to cut your food because that would be violence?"

"Just get in the car."

Over lunch, we gossiped about a conceited TV producer who had once badgered Susie into bed and a blow job, acting as if he was some incredible Casanova. He wasn't, and he had a small penis.

"Was it short but fat like a beer can, Susie?" Andrew asked.

Susie shook her head back and forth, barely able to talk she was laughing so hard. "I'm not telling!"

"Then just show us," Jon said. "Was it like this?" — he made a very small O with his lips — "Or like this?" — and he stretched his mouth open wide. I spit out my food.

After the jokes subsided I turned to Andrew and asked him The Question.

"So, what do you do?"

"I'm a writer."

Naturally I followed with "What do you write about?"

He told me that, right now, he was on his way to San Francisco to start writing an adventure travel guide to northern California, but he used to be an investigative reporter down in Santa Barbara and that's how he met Susie.

"She was one of the speakers at the university's conference on censorship and pornography. I interviewed her." He kept eating. "I thought she was such a cool person and I liked what she had to say about sex. So we became friends."

I was silent for a second a two, sucking intently on the straw leading into my iced tea and raising one eyebrow, trying to think of something witty to say, but I waited too long.

"Hey, Action Figure!" Susie stuck her arm out across the table and waved to get Andrew's attention. "Jon wants you to take him surfing. He's never been!"

We went to check the surf at Pleasure Point. Laura rode with me since Susie was late for an appointment and had to leave. Jon went in Andrew's Chevy Blazer, which was crammed full of wetsuits, surfboards, a mountain bike, backpacks, snorkeling gear, tents, a spear gun, the works of Carl Jung and a large chocolate Labrador named Molly, as well as a collection of wadded-up garbage from every previous adventure he'd ever had.

"Are you a surfer?" I asked Laura.

"God, no. I'm into lethargy." She laughed.

"How long have you and Andrew been together?"

"All my life. He's my brother."

"Oh."

According to Andrew, the surf looked small but good, and he and Jon were having gear talk when I interrupted. "What about me? I want to go, too." I knew almost nothing about surfing except that it involved a surfboard and the ocean. In fact, when it comes to the athletic/outdoor life, I am naturally giftless. I cannot throw, catch or even keep score for any game that involves a ball. I have a debilitating fear of heights, dislike for speed, terrible hand-eye coordination and a fear of all animals. But I love the ocean and surfing looked fun. *I can swim. How hard can it be?*

Just getting down to the beach nearly killed me. Not only did it require a climb down a rocky cliff — okay, so it was a *small* cliff — but I had to do it while carrying nine feet of fiberglass. Andrew and Jon skipped down the trail. I stood at the top, sweating over my first step.

"I'll carry the board down," Andrew called and came back up to retrieve it. Then he came to retrieve me, as I ungracefully slid and clawed and scrambled my way down, ass first.

Eventually all three of us were in waist-high water, boards floating at our sides. "Now we're going to paddle out past the shorebreak to the peak," Andrew instructed. Jon instinctively lay down on his board and began paddling through the churning white foam to where the ridable waves break. Andrew was off and paddling too, but I wasn't going anywhere. Every time I'd try to punch through one of the little incoming waves, it would break right on my head, throw me off the board and spit me back to shore, where I took a nice beating against the rocks. After I had choked on countless mouthfuls of saltwater and even been slapped in the face by my board, Andrew surfed back in and shouted, "Grab my leash and I'll pull you out!" So I lunged for the thin plastic cord that linked Andrew's board to his ankle and held on.

"You did good," Andrew said when we reached calmer water.

"Yeah, right." I was insanely blinking my eyes to make sure my contact lenses hadn't floated away and checking for any loose snot that might be hanging out of my nose.

"Okay, you sucked." Andrew laughed. "But you'll do better next time. Most people don't even get this far. I think you're courageous."

My courageous objectives were as follows: to stop thinking a shark was attacking me whenever I felt a piece of kelp touch my foot, to sit on the surfboard without falling off and to stay out of people's way as they came ripping past me. Jon was

more adventurous, catching a few waves and dropping in on —
crashing into, actually — local surf legend Wingnut, the star
of the film *Endless Summer 2*. Andrew stuck by us, patiently
filling us in on the complex etiquette of surf culture, explaining
the fundamentals of wave dynamics and leading by example.
I watched him drop in on wave after wave, and ride them for
what seemed like forever. He made it look so easy.

About two hours later, my body and ego sufficiently bruised
from countless wipeouts, we decided to paddle in. An intricate
what-to-do-next plan was being discussed but I suddenly felt
feverish, so I headed back to Susie's for a hot shower where,
from her seat on the toilet, she demanded to know every detail.
Was the water cold? Freezing. Did you catch a wave? No. Were
you scared? Terrified. How did Jon do? Good. What do you
think of Andrew?

"I think Andrew's great. He's cute, smart, funny, extremely
patient. How old is he, anyway?"

"Twenty-seven, I think."

"Wow, he looks older. I mean, he *acts* older. Wiser. Anyway, too bad for me he's a fag."

"A fag? What are you talking about? He's totally into girls!"

I groaned like a girl who just dropped her ice cream cone
and yanked the shower curtain back. "I just spent the entire
time cruising all the other guys in the water, especially this
one black surfer dude. I kept saying things like 'Isn't he hot?'
or 'What about him?' I thought Andrew and I were bond-
ing — in a homo way."

"You what?" Susie was incredulous.

"How the hell was I supposed to know he's straight?" I
snapped. "Here's a good-looking, single guy with a classic buzz
cut and a neatly trimmed goatee and a raised sexual conscious-

ness who's rendezvousing with queer sex guru *Susie Bright* on his way up to *San Francisco*. When Laura told me she was his *sister,* I assumed he was gay."

I looked at my feet and watched the hot water swirl down the drain. *So what if I crushed all potential? Not that there was any potential anyway, since I couldn't possibly have looked uglier today or been more of a dork at surfing. Besides, I am embracing solitude. I have solemnly vowed to remain a free agent. I am going to be alone and like it.*

After dinner, I decided to lie in bed and read. I had just switched off the light when Susie came into the room and we started talking in the dark, on the futon, on the floor. Then Andrew — *oh, he's back* — came in and we all started talking in the dark, on the futon, on the floor. Soon Andrew and I were engaged in a kind of soft hand dance, letting our fingers trace up and down each other's arms. Susie said goodnight. I was about to say that if there wasn't another bed available in the house, he could share mine — strictly a platonic offer — but before I could say a word he was kissing me, deeply. And soon, he was doing more than that.

The next morning Andrew and I were under the covers kissing and I felt the eerie sensation that we were being watched. I popped my head out and saw five-year-old Aretha Bright in her Pocahontas nightgown staring down at us.

"Is Andrew a handsome prince?" she asked. And because I thought she was so adorable in the way that only little girls can be, and because it was early and I was sleepy and, well, the whole thing did seem remarkably fantastic, I said yes.

In the afternoon we drove up to San Francisco together and I invited Andrew to stay at my apartment. For the next few days, every drop of our time was consumed fucking and feeding and counting the stars in each other's eyes. Crazy how a person can pop into your life one day, quite by accident, and completely transform it. Seventy-two hours after meeting Andrew, I was in a state of reckless transport, pitched a million miles an hour with all the dials set on high. I'd sworn to myself I would use caution the next time around — but here I was, falling. And for the first time in my life, the uncertainty of it all terrified me. The thought of Andrew being just another fleeting romance was unbearable, and I actually considered ending things right then and there, to avoid the inevitable crash-and-burn twenty months down the road — or two weeks for all I knew — but now *that* seemed foolish. I compromised: a light tap on the brakes.

"I promised my friend Ron that I'd spend the Fourth of July with him at his ranch in Ukiah," I told Andrew the next morning when we were lying in bed. "I'll be back in two days, but I made these plans so I really should go."

"Hurry back, okay?" He kissed me.

I drove up to Ukiah, a small town about 120 miles north of San Francisco, and found Ron suffering from a terrible case of poison oak. He was miserable, which made me miserable, and we basically spent the day insulting each other, just like old times. The following morning at seven, the phone rang.

"It's Susie." Ron poked me and held out the cordless phone. I grabbed it.

"Hello?" Susie started talking but I was distracted because Ron just stood there, scratching his poison oak and eavesdropping. "Hang on a second." I got out of bed and walked outside, onto the deck. "Sorry. Ron was spying on me, as usual. Go on."

"I said, what have you done to Andrew?"

"What? Is something wrong? Is he sick?"

"Yeah, lovesick. He called me last night out of his mind over you, crazy with longing and fear of the unknown. He wanted to make sure you weren't a love-'em-and-leave-'em kind of girl."

Jon picked up the extension. "Your planets have collided," he insisted. "He's the man!"

So. Andrew's serious about me. That little bit of information certainly gave me the advantage.

When I got back to San Francisco, Andrew and I went to Ocean Beach, to go surfing. Ocean Beach is typically a fierce place. Riptides, undertows, howling winds, monster waves and icy gray water all blanketed in bone-chilling fog. On rare days, though, it's warm and sunny, and the ocean looks as if it's made of glass. This was one of those days.

"There's less beach here than I remember," I said.

"That's because the tide is high."

"Oh." I gave him a quizzical look.

"You know, the tide goes in and out twice a day."

I had to confess that no, I didn't know. "I feel so stupid. I grew up in a big, landlocked city and I don't know much about the ocean or the wilderness and, honestly, I'm scared of it. I never even had any pets — well, I take that back. I had a guinea pig once and it went stir crazy from being in its cage and it bit me. That's what I learned growing up — all of nature is out to attack and kill me! I mean, I'll ride the subway through the Bronx at three A.M. before I'll walk alone through the forest at night. I've never been camping, I've never taken a shit in the woods, I didn't even know that salmon swim back upstream to spawn and die until a few years ago — in fact, an old boyfriend basically broke up with me over my salmon ignorance. He was appalled, and kept saying, 'I can't believe you don't know about salmon.' Anyway, I thought you should know that I'm not exactly Jane Goodall."

"Lisa." He reached out and touched my cheek. "That doesn't matter. Believe me, there are plenty of things that terrify me, things that you seem to handle with such ease and finesse." He paused, and tucked one of my stray hairs behind my ear. "Sometimes I think my action figure persona is a way for me to hide from my own fears. The fears that are more emotional than physical."

That afternoon, I caught my first wave. I didn't stand up, just rode it in on my belly, arms outstretched like a flying superhero. I loved the taste of salt on my face and in my mouth, the way it made my hair sticky and me feel so connected to the earth. Between waves, Andrew explained what a riptide is, the many commercial uses for kelp and how to tell the difference between a shark and a dolphin when you see a fin in the water.

"Sharks zig and zag. Dolphins go up and down, in and out of the water."

Sitting on my surfboard and listening, I felt tears start to well up.

"What?" He scrutinized my face.

"I'm in awe over your mastery of the natural world."

"I don't have mastery over it." He smiled. "Just a good working relationship."

There's a pureness about him, I thought, a rare honesty and goodness that falls all around him and sparkles like a halo. And when, on the twelfth day, he told me he loved me, something inside me said, *This is it.*

"Why didn't Susie introduce us sooner?" I wondered out loud.

"Well, I did ask about you. I remember Susie showing me your picture and telling me that you'd just gotten this book deal and were planning to spend your advance holed up in a fancy hotel room with gigolos and a ghostwriter —"

"— If only I'd stuck with the plan, my book would have been written by now!"

"— So I said, 'Give her my number! She could kill two birds with one stone.' But Susie said, 'No, Lisa's not into hairy guys.'"

"Oh, how wrong I was." I ran my fingers through his fur and rubbed my nose in his beard. His smell intoxicated me and all I wanted to do was be close to him, kiss his toes, marvel over his long eyelashes and objectify his perfect ass while he walked around the house naked. And so, that was all I did.

Week after week, work came to a standstill. Every morning, I'd wake up with the best intentions of getting down to business and ended up barely writing a paragraph. Falling in love is the worst obstacle to writing. When I was angry and depressed, I churned out hundreds of pages of scintillating prose. Now I couldn't pick up a pen without a big string of drool sliding off the end of it. Andrew's professional progress wasn't much better, and we took turns warding off the particularly distressing brand of anxiety that comes from not writing.

"How am I supposed to plumb the depths of my soul when I'm on cloud sixty-nine?"

"Relax, this is research," Andrew said, feeding me *tekka maki* while I soaked in the tub that he filled for me. "If you hadn't fallen in love with me, you wouldn't have a happy ending for your book."

Five months after we met, Andrew and I found a house in San Francisco and officially moved in together. Over the course of our courtship, Aretha continued to insist that Andrew was a handsome prince. She'd point to his picture on the refrigerator and say, "Here he is, Andrew the Handsome Prince. He's a handsome prince, right?" It was part of her larger obsession with fairy princesses and fancy gowns and romance. All this from a girl who's been raised by the bisexual, nonmonogamous, politically radical Susie Sexpert.

"He certainly is handsome, isn't he?" I'd say and let it go. This time I felt obligated to be honest because I knew that even the most handsome of all princes are only human.

"You guys are gonna get married." She giggled.

"Oh, you think so?" I teased her. I was beginning to think the same thing myself.

• • •

I grew up listening to my mother tell the story over and over of how she wanted to run away on her wedding day because she didn't love my father. But it was 1945 and the world was at war and pickings were slim. Besides, my father loved her so much my mother believed she would grow to love him. I suppose she did, but their marriage was more nightmare than fairy tale.

The idea of motherhood has always come easy to me, but the idea of marriage has not. As a little girl I loved the idea of the fancy dress and a big party, but I was never crazy about the husband part. In college, I fell out of love with The Dress and swore that if by some slim chance I ever got married, I would never wear a bride costume, much less a white one that symbolized virginity. The consumerist bridal industry made me sick with its Most Important Day of Your Life propaganda: You deserve the most expensive frills, so pay no attention to our price-gouging! As for marriage itself, what a prison. I could rant about the cruelties women endured as wives for hours. Foot-binding in China, bride burning in India, and the good old American tradition of wives as trophies, breeders, pieces of property.

Eventually I became less of a hothead around the word *marriage*, but I remained skeptical. I couldn't shake the feeling that marriage was still a socially celebrated form of slavery. I didn't want to sacrifice my life to good housekeeping or end up being a mommy to a grown man. I couldn't stand the thought of being Mrs. So-and-So. I didn't want to lose my identity or, worse, my mind. In this respect, I certainly agreed with Betty Dodson: Two hearts beat as one, the total merger of two beings, loss of self — yippee for love! Yet I longed to be in love with a man and raise a family together. I didn't know what to call that. A pair bond? A love alliance? I imagined being in a sort of Simone de Beauvoir/Jean-Paul Sartre relationship — but with kids. My man and I might live separately, take other lovers if need be, share career and parenting responsibilities equally, but most of all, cultivate an intensely passionate and primary devotion to each other, till death do us part.

Flashback: By the time Ron Gompertz proposed to me, I felt pretty confident that I wouldn't end up contracting mad-housewife disease. I worked hard at carving out my independent life, even harder at preserving it, and believed I had the strength and skills to keep it up. Instead of avoiding marriage, I wanted to redefine it — the same way I'd chosen to redefine, say, pornography — and experience it on my own terms. It was a decision encouraged, in no small part, by Ron's favorite adage: "If you hate elevator music, make elevator music."

Our marriage plan was more an act of efficiency rather than romance, so at that point you'd think we'd just swing by the courthouse and tie the knot. But no. I wanted a big party. I wanted to wear The Dress. My sudden craving for convention bewildered many, including me: If I hated tradition so much, why did I want a traditional wedding? "Because I just want it, that's why!" From my cornered position that was the only answer I could give.

And so Ron and I fought. We fought about the venue, the caterers, the flowers, the invitations, the photographer, the band, my dress, his suit and, most important, the price tag of it all. We fought until I threw the ring back in anger. The following week we both accepted the truth: The problem wasn't our wedding, it was our marriage. It would never be right, never in a million years, and we had to move on.

In the calm after the storm, I began to see why I wanted The Dress and the party: I valued the ritual and tradition of celebrating love more than I ever allowed myself to admit. In my fast-paced postmodern world, there seemed to be so few rituals left, and I felt the need to experience the one that was, really, about love. Forget low-key — I wanted pomp and circumstance! Bring on the champagne toasts, the fluffy cake, the conga line! Shout about it from the highest mountaintop! And yes, bring on The Dress. Nobody believes a white gown symbolizes virginity anymore. These days The Dress is about beauty and its ability to make any woman — or man — who wears it feel like a princess.

Even though my own wedding plans were kaput, my appreciation for the ritual kept growing. When my friends Paul Kimball and Laura Beatty asked me if I'd perform their wedding ceremony, I was flattered and delighted, but unsure about the logistics.

"Does this mean I need to mail in five bucks and get one of those phony minister certificates?" I laughed.

"Actually, you're required to sign the marriage license, so you'll need bona fide credentials," Laura told me.

Laura hooked me up with Seth Katz, a cultural Jew raised by radical atheist intellectuals, who was a minister of the Universal Life Church and had performed several weddings. "All you have to do to become a minister is ask — send in your name and address on a piece of paper and it's official," he said. So I did.

The cover of the pamphlet I received, along with my minister's certificate, featured a drawing of the American flag and the group's life-affirming trinity — "Freedom, Food, Sexuality. Heaven is when you have it. Hell is when you don't" — along with little descriptions of why freedom, food and sex, in that order, are so important. The doctrine of the ULC is a fast read, since there's only one: "We only believe in that which is right! Every person has the right to interpret what is right for themselves, as long as it doesn't interfere with the rights of others." It's a philosophy that even the biggest heretic can support. Opposite a cut-and-paste collage of church founder the Reverend Kirby Hensley is a list of other ULC ministers, including Hugh Hefner, Debbie Reynolds, Lawrence Welk, and the Rolling Stones.

On April Fool's Day, 1995, I married Laura and Paul in his parents' backyard. It was a small, elegant affair. She wore a simple white dress, he wore a suit and so did I. The following April, I married another couple, my friends Joy and Michael. Theirs was a traditional blowout: big white dress, huge bridal party and four generations of relatives packing the dance floor. Their styles were different but the importance they placed on the marriage contract itself was exactly the same. Each wanted a ceremony that was awe-inspiring but not drippy, spiritual but not religious, whimsical but not absurd and, above all, expressive of their history with each other and the integrity of their commitment. We all knew couples who ended up in tears during their wedding ceremony — not out of joy but because some bozo bureaucrat got their names wrong or an aloof clergy member rattled off the most boring, soulless platitudes. Why settle for empty formalities when you can have your ritual of love conducted by someone who really loves you?

Suddenly it seemed as if everyone was taking the plunge in their own distinct way. My lesbian friends Jackie and Shar got hitched in a body modification parlor and had their rings tattooed on. Annie Sprinkle sent me a wedding announcement with a photo of her and her wife in matching, frilly wedding dresses, tits exposed. I got so inspired about Marriage: The Latest Thing that I pitched the story to an editor at the *LA Times*. A few days later he responded, saying that the bunch of aging hippies who make up the editorial board felt that everything I had to say about marriage had already been said in the sixties.

Now, do poets stop writing about sunsets because we've all seen thousands of them? Do musicians stop playing in the key of G just because we've all heard it before? I think not. Love, baby, makes the world go around. Every generation searches for its own heroes, reinvents the rules and writes its own love stories.

•••

To celebrate Andrew's twenty-eighth year, we flew to New York City. It was his first trip to Manhattan, a birthday gift from me. It had been one year since Andrew and I met. We stayed with my friend Dan, as I always did, and I threw Andrew a small surprise party in his apartment. The next day over lunch at the Bowery Bar he said, "Now I've got a surprise for you." We got on the B train and headed uptown.

"This train ends up in Queens, you know. Are you sure we're going the right way?"

"Positive." He smiled. Inside me, a small ping of disappointment. I'd hoped the surprise might be shoe shopping in SoHo.

We got off at 72nd Street and headed into Central Park, towards the lake. "A boat ride?"

Andrew grabbed my hand and kissed it. "Smarty."

Once in the rowboat, off came his shoes, his shirt. I leaned back, feeling glamorous in my Italian sunglasses and lipstick under a hot blue June sky, watching his muscles work as he rowed. Every stroke of the oar sent a ripple down his perfect, perfect abs. The dark hair on his chest glistened with the dew of sweat, his scent was in the air and I thought, *He is so fucking beautiful.* Andrew smoothly pulled us past the logjam of incompetents, who couldn't figure out how to get their boat going in any direction, and into the open water. *Impressive.*

Under the bridge and around two swans, we stopped in front of the Dakota, the famous building where John and Yoko once lived, and drifted.

"Are you having a good time?" he asked.

"Great time."

"Good, because I've got something important to ask you." He got down on his knees in the sloppy water in the bottom of the boat. "Lisa, will you marry me?"

"Oh, Andrew," I whispered. My jaw dropped. *So this is the surprise.* I hung there, milking time for every ounce of sensation in between the question and the answer.

"Uh . . . you should really say something," he said, nervously.

"Yes, yes, yes, OH YES!" was, of course, my response. Andrew reached out and took off my sunglasses. He took my face in his hands and kissed my wet eyes, my cheeks, my mouth. And there we were, surrounded by our own private corona, oblivious to everything else.

• • •

"I was right!" Laura Miller said when I called to tell her about the engagement and our ring shopping adventure down Fifth Avenue. "He's the Marlboro Man."

"Except he doesn't smoke." I laughed.

In the months preceding the wedding, the best wishes came rolling in, along with a coy curiosity about our sex life. An old acquaintance came up to Andrew on the street and said, "Hey, man, I hear you're marrying a porn star!" Another asked if Andrew was afraid of being "tied down."

"So what did you say?" I asked.

"I told him, 'No way! Lisa's all ball and no chain.'"

When I told people I was getting married, I was often tempted to add the disclaimer, "But it's not what you think!" While there are many definitions of marriage, the American universal is this: Marriage means having sex with the same person and only that person for the REST OF YOUR LIFE.

My friends wondered how Andrew and I were handling the monogamy issue: Was it going to be an "open" marriage? Or were we choosing to be only with each other? What if one of us had a one-night stand — would we be absolutely discreet or tell all? How about a ménage à trois? Anonymous phone sex? Cybersex? Did any of that figure into our plans? The most truthful answer I could give was "It depends."

"But what if Andrew cheated on you?" my friend Alex asked. "How would you feel?"

"It depends on how you define cheating," I said.

As a kid I listened to song after song on the radio about the evils of cheating, like Hendrix's "Hey, Joe" where Joe kills his old lady for messing around with another man, and I always thought, *These people are really overreacting.* Through the years, I've seen people try to stick to all kinds of intricate definitions for fidelity. It isn't cheating if we just kiss. If I let her blow me but don't do anything to her. If we're only typing dirty words to each other online. But to me, cheating is not the degree of the sex act, it's when you feel that you have to lie. When you've lost the courage to tell your lover the truth about what you've done because you know it would destroy things, and that sick, guilty feeling won't stop jabbing you in the gut — that's cheating. And it is the worst kind of betrayal.

Fidelity — what it means and how it works in theory versus practice over time — is extremely complex. Everyday people enter into committed relationships thinking they will never, ever even *look* at another person. Others find monogamy confining and possessive, and think jealousy is something they've outgrown. And you know what? All too often we end up surprised and devastated by the lizard-brain impulses we thought we had trained so well.

It was impossible for me to predict how I would feel about a specific instance that hadn't even happened yet — context, after all, is everything — but I was unequivocal on three things. One: Fidelity does not preclude sexual adventure. It is completely possible to be devoted to your partner and make room for erotic dalliances. Two: Emotional fidelity means more to me than sexual fidelity. All sorts of outside influences pose threats to a love relationship — work, demanding friendships, the need to climb Mount Everest — many of which can be far more damaging than the urge for sexual variety. Fidelity is not simply where you stick your tongue, it's where you lay down your heart. Fidelity is a promise of faithfulness in the greatest sense; a commitment to love and cherish each other above all others. Three: I loved my fiancé very, very much and was ready to make that lifelong promise to be true.

•••

"No naked men jumping out of cakes, no strippers, no sex," I told Susie. As Best Babe (Matron of Honor is so horribly dowdy) the important duty of organizing the bachelorette party fell to her. "This is not the Last Chance Ranch where I get my sexual ya-yas out before the door slams shut."

"Got it."

"So?"

"We could build a menstrual hut."

"Too goal-oriented."

"Then how about some kind of beach party, beauty-parloring, cocktail-shakin', consciousness-raising experience?"

"Totally."

The weekend before the wedding, Andrew went on a back-country bike trip with his buddies in the Santa Ynez mountains to swill and grill around the campfire. I headed out to the all-day, all-night, all-girl extravaganza hosted by Susie and my dear friend Joy Johnson. Friends arrived from all four corners of the States — San Francisco, Miami, New York, Los Angeles — about twelve in all, to celebrate. We picnicked at the beach, we hung out *chez* Bright, ordered in facials and massages and soaked in the hot tub. We ate pâté, drank the finest martinis, gabbed and blabbed and spun stories that had us cracking up and breaking down like old cronies, even though many of my friends had never met each other before. For the grand finale, my friend Dorothy broke out her electric guitar and played "Stairway to Heaven," with me, of course, doing Robert Plant to her Jimmy Page. The rest of the party jammed along on congas, recorders, triangles and maracas.

• • •

Andrew and I were married on April 25, 1997, in the sunken garden of the Santa Barbara courthouse, a beautiful Spanish Revival masterpiece built in the 1930s. Seventy-five degrees and not a cloud in the sky. I wore a 1940s ivory silk and tulle dress with a five-foot train and a short veil my in-laws helped me make. Andrew wore a three-button navy suit and a white gardenia. I walked down the aisle to Wagner's Wedding March and almost — almost! — made it through my vows without crying.

Even though Andrew and I read our vows to each other prior to the ceremony so there'd be no surprises — and I'd certainly made all sorts of intimate declarations in public before — nothing could have prepared me for what happened when I said those words in front of the people who make up our lives. To look out into the crowd and see our parents, our families, our friends, over one hundred people from completely different walks of life who'd never been together before and probably never will be again, crying with joy and radiating love for me and Andrew was one of the most overwhelming sensations I've ever experienced. The energy was so intense, I felt suspended in a forcefield of love, awestruck by the power of this ritual.

Dinner and dancing took place in a hall right on the beach, as the sun set over the Pacific. Two cheesy plastic surfers, a boy and a girl, graced the top of our wedding cake. A Cuban salsa band played while my brother Bud passed out the fancy cigars. The evening ended with a couple of standbys: the garter and bouquet toss.

Single guys still dig the garter toss. Maybe it's the stripper music or the glimpse up the bride's dress, but it always draws a crowd. The bouquet toss, however, has definitely lost its appeal. I remember weddings where single women shoved and elbowed and practically clawed each others' eyes out trying to grab the thing in hopes that they would be the next bride. But now? I might as well have been throwing a grenade. The dance floor was empty and only after some prodding did a handful of women drag themselves out there, trying to look enthusiastic. My first throw hit the ceiling beams, so a retoss was demanded. The second time, we had a winner: Greg Graeff, my old porndog boyfriend. He was sitting at a table behind the bouquet line, and when the flowers sailed over the heads of the nonplussed, Greg, at six foot four, stood up and snagged them. He cuddled the bouquet in his arms like a baby and smiled like Miss America as the flashbulbs went off. It couldn't have fallen to a more qualified contestant. "I hate to think the pony ride is over at thirty-six," he'd confided earlier. "But at this point in my life, I'm not looking to get laid. I'm looking for my wife."

But the elders weren't pleased with this modern twist so I threw the bouquet a third time. An already-engaged-to-be-married woman caught it but the long stem jabbed her in the face. The next day, she had a black eye. Tradition, after all, can be a dangerous thing.

Epilogue

"**H**EY, ISN'T THIS the book you read as a kid?" We were hanging out in a used bookstore, and Andrew was holding up an old paperback copy of *Everything You Always Wanted to Know About Sex — But Were Afraid to Ask* as explained by David Reuben, M.D.

"Oh my God, yes! I've gotta have it." I had lost my copy in 1975.

"Anything for you, my darling wife."

Andrew carried the book up to the checkout counter — along with his own selections: *Running the Amazon* and *The Control of Nature* — where he paid two bucks for it, five cents more than it cost back when it was first published in 1969.

We walked to a café, ordered a couple of beers and took turns reading out loud from the sex book. This book was a bestseller in its day, one of the first mass-market publications to deal frankly with the sticky subject of sex. It's arranged as a series of questions and answers, and it includes straightforward chapters on male and female anatomy, masturbation, sexual intercourse, prostitution, menopause, VD, abortion before it was legal and so on. A chapter titled "September Sex" even explains how senior citizens with arthritis get it on. While its goal is to provide information and steer clear of moral judgments, many of the "facts" are so clearly biased by today's standards that Andrew and I couldn't stop laughing.

"'If oral sex is a prelude to intercourse,'" I read with a professorial tone, "'it's hard to find anything harmful or wrong about it.'"

"But what if it isn't a prelude to intercourse?"

"A-ha! That's the very next question! Unless you are a man with a spinal injury or a woman with cancer, it says you may have an emotional problem."

The lowdown on homosexuality was particularly infuriating. "Check this out," Andrew said. "'Basically all homosexuals are alike — looking for love where there can be no love and looking for sexual satisfaction where there can be no lasting satisfaction.'"

Our favorite chapter, naturally, was "Sexual Perversion."

"I want to see what it says about S/M," and I reached out to grab the book.

"Uh, uh, uh!" Andrew pulled the book away from me and held it over his head. "Let me read it," he said, flipping the pages. "S/M, here called 'S and M,' is something only gay men practice."

"No way!"

"It says that S and M's are the cruelest people on earth. 'In ancient times they found employment as professional torturers and executioners. More recently they filled the ranks of Hitler's Gestapo and SS.' "

"Let me see that!" And sure enough, he wasn't kidding. So much for the good old days.

It's been fourteen years since that vibrator leapt from the closet and bonked me on the head. Never in my wildest dreams could I have pictured where the inspiration would take me. I never imagined that I would help build the genre now called Women's Erotica, or take part in shaping sexual democracy on the digital frontier. And I certainly never believed I would get mail from my mother addressed to Mrs. Andrew Rice, the envelope decorated with religious affirmations, and think it was cute.

As I turn this thing called sex around in my hand like a prism and watch the light reflect in unexpected directions, my final conclusion is this: I *have* evolved. And America has evolved as a culture, a group. Not in a straight line toward perfection, but then that's not the way evolution works. Evolution is random and sloppy. We take two steps forward and one step back. Just when we break free of old adversities, we're hit with a new plague. We tear off our clothes, then hurry to get dressed. All the answers only seem to raise more questions. More than one person has told me that if I keep talking about sex, I'll take all the mystery out of it. But the mystery is endless, and that's what keeps me going.